ADVENTURE TIME™

CARD WARS

Official Guide

CARTOON NETWORK BOOKS
Penguin Young Readers Group
An Imprint of Penguin Random House LLC

Published in 2016 by Cartoon Network Books, an imprint of Penguin Random House LLC, 345 Hudson Street, New York, New York 10014. Manufactured in China.

ISBN 9780399541636                                    10 9 8 7 6 5 4 3 2 1

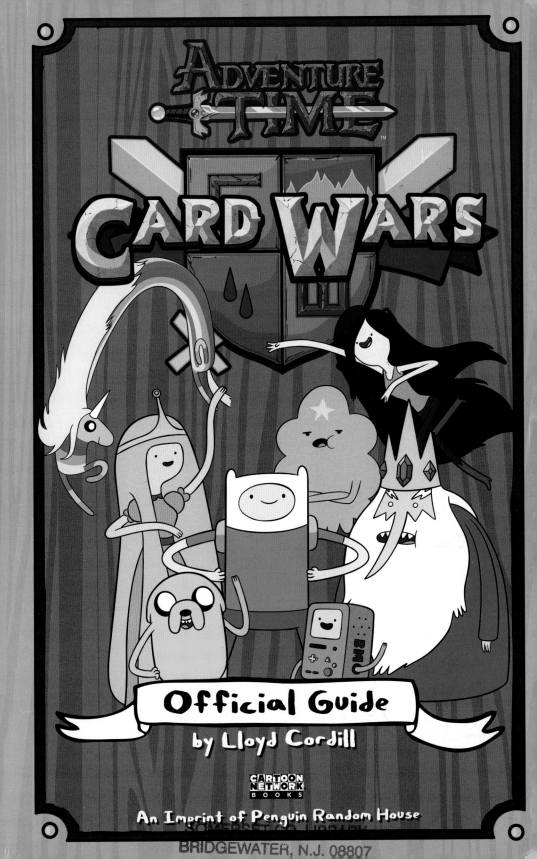

# ADVENTURE TIME

# CARD WARS

## Official Guide

by Lloyd Cordill

CARTOON NETWORK BOOKS

An Imprint of Penguin Random House

# Table of Contents

# INTRODUCTION

## CARD WARS! THE AWESOMEST FANTASY CARD GAME IN THE LAND OF OOO.

IN THE PAGES OF THIS ANCIENT TOME, YOU WILL LEARN THE SECRETS OF THIS EPIC AND TOTALLY RAD GAME. SO SUMMON YOUR FRIENDS AND FORM A GATHERING, FOR YOU WILL GO ON TO GREAT THINGS ONCE YOU LEARN THE CARDS, MASTER THE TACTICS, AND HONE THE SKILLS NECESSARY TO BECOME THE ULTIMATE CARD WARS PLAYER!

Yeah, yeah, yeah, ancient tome or whatever. Listen up, dudes and dudettes! You don't need some fancy encyclopedia to become a Card Wars genie-us like old Jake. You just need a few pointers from me and my compadres. Get ready. We're about to drop some knowledge, Card Wars–style!

Card Wars is a "Lane Combat Trading Card Game." That means you command superstrong Creatures, cast powerful Spells, and go head to head against your opponent's troops! In this guide, you'll learn how to use, mix, and power up the following decks:

Finn vs. Jake Collector's Pack
BMO vs. Lady Rainicorn Collector's Pack
Princess Bubblegum vs. Lumpy Space Princess Collector's Pack
Ice King vs. Marceline Collector's Pack
Lemongrab vs. Gunter Collector's Pack
Fionna vs. Cake Collector's Pack
For the Glory! Booster Pack

Each set comes with a copy of the SUPER COMPLICATED RULES. Go ahead and read the rule book first! That way, everything written in here won't look like gobbledygook. Oh—and in case you don't recognize a card, just look for it in the back of the book so you can find out which pack it came from.

Now get ready to Floop it up!

Card Wars is a game about making decisions, and you make the most important decision before the game even starts: What kind of deck do you want to play? The type of deck is determined by your Landscapes. Each Landscape offers a different style of play, so pick your favorite! If you can't choose, turn to page 154 for a quiz that will tell you what deck best fits your personality.

Your choice of Landscapes also decides what cards you can play in your deck.

Landscape

Cornfield

© 2013 Cryptozoic Entertainment    TM & © Cartoon Network. (s13)

See that symbol in the upper right corner of each card? That tells you what type of Landscape you need to control in order to play the card. The number in the upper left corner tells you how many Actions it costs to play the card. **Field Stalker** costs 1 Action. **Cornataur** costs 2 Actions. But there's more! That number also tells you how many Landscapes of that type you need to control to play the card. Field Stalker requires 1 Cornfield Landscape. Cornataur requires 2 Cornfield Landscapes. If, for some reason, one of your Landscapes gets flipped facedown, be careful! You might not be able to play some of your Creatures.

Pro tip! If you have a mixed-Landscape deck, your Creatures aren't limited to the Lanes that match their Landscape type. You can play a NiceLands Creature onto a Useless Swamp Landscape, as long as you control enough NiceLands Landscapes to cover the Action cost.

### CORNFIELD:

Cornfield decks are some of the most aggressive in Card Wars. The Creatures are cheap and have high Attack (ATK). Many Corn Creatures get additional strength and abilities for each Cornfield Landscape you have.

### BLUE PLAINS:

Blue Plains decks are some of the most challenging decks to play. They have lots of utility Creatures with Floop abilities that allow you to eke out incremental value—that means a little bit of advantage at a time. Blue Plains decks are also the best at drawing cards, and require the use of multi-card combos to succeed.

### USELESS SWAMP:

Useless Swamp decks focus on the discard pile. Useless Swamp Creatures get super powerful if you have enough cards in your discard pile. Some Spells and Floop abilities even let you put cards from your discard pile into your hand.

# SANDYLANDS:

SandyLands decks are aggressive and feature Creatures that have powerful effects when they enter play. The decks use Spells and Floop abilities that return Creatures to your hand, so you can play them again!

# NICELANDS:

NiceLands decks have Creatures that are cute as cupcakes (and some literal cupcakes) and that care about how much Damage is on them. After taking a few hits, NiceLands Creatures can get superstrong. These decks combo with Spells and abilities that Damage their own Creatures to speed up this process.

# ICYLANDS:

IcyLands decks are freezing, but they sure don't move at glacial speed. IcyLands Creatures hit hard and fast, and get stronger if your opponent doesn't have a Creature in the same Lane. IcyLands decks also use Frozen tokens to slow their opponents' progress.

**RAINBOW** cards are wild cards. They aren't attached to any specific Landscape, so you can play them in any deck! More about these magical cards later.

The goal of the game is to reduce your opponent's Hit Points from 25 to 0. Simple, right? If you can do that, then you win! The winner of Card Wars is the Cool Guy, and the loser is a Dweeb.

## Parts of a Card

1. **Name of Card**—This is the card's name. It's usually something super cool.
2. **Action Cost**—The number of Actions it takes to play this card. If it's not a Rainbow card, you need at least this number of Landscapes of the given type to play this card.
3. **Landscape Type**—The type of Landscape this card is (Cornfield, NiceLands, etc.).
4. **Art**—Beauty is in the eye of the beholder. And this art is in the eye of you!
5. **Card Type**—The card's Landscape type, as well as its card type (Creature, Spell, or Building).
6. **Game Text**—The effects of the card will be here.
7. **Attack (ATK)**—The amount of Damage the Creature will do in combat, either to the opponent or the other Creature in this Lane.
8. **Defense (DEF)**—The amount of Damage this Creature can take before it is discarded.

There are three positions your cards can be in at any point.

**Ready:** This is your normal, upright, ready-for-anything position. Remember to move your cards back to Ready at the beginning of every turn. Some cards even have special abilities that only apply to Ready cards.

**Flooped:** To Floop, turn your card sideways and move it to the bottom of the Landscape, over the text. This shows that you're activating the card's special Floop ability, and that it won't be going into the Fight phase.

**Fight:** To Activate your Creature to Fight, turn your card sideways and move it to the top of the Landscape. Then Attack!

If your Creatures are in the Flooped or Fight position, they are also considered "exhausted." Can you blame them? Card Warring is hard work!

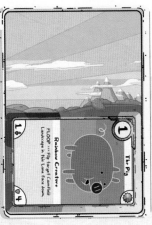

**Ready**    **Flooped**    **Fight**

## Set-Up Sequence

# Here are the steps to take at the beginning of each game.

1. Choose a deck

2. Place your Landscapes on the table

3. Decide who goes first

4. Shuffle your deck and draw 5 cards

5. Do you like your hand of cards? If not, you may re-draw your hand one time only

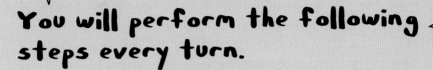

## Turn Sequence

You will perform the following steps every turn.

1. Ready all your cards

2. Draw a card

3. You have 2 Actions to spend

4. Do you want to Floop?

5. Do you want to spend 1 Action to draw a card?

6. Fight!

7. End of turn

Steps 3, 4, and 5 may be performed in any order. The order in which you perform these moves is called *sequencing*, and it's one of the most important strategic components of Card Wars. Sequence your plays correctly, and you will maximize your potential!

> Remember! Refer to the *Adventure Time Card Wars Rule Book* for more detailed instructions on how to play Card Wars!

Card Wars is a game about resources. And one of your most important resources is Actions! You only get 2 Actions per turn, so you gotta think hard about how to spend them.

You can use Actions to play Creature or Building cards from your hand. This **Bog Frog Bomb** Creature costs 2 Actions, and goes directly onto the Landscape.

This **Mausoleum** Building costs 1 Action, and goes below it.

You can use Actions to play Spell cards from your hand. This **Cerebral Bloodstorm** Spell costs 1 Action. Spell cards are one-time use (unless your deck has the savvy to revive them).

This Creature, **The Pig**, costs 1 Action to play. The Pig also has a Floop ability, but using a Floop ability does not cost any Actions. You can Floop at any point during the Action sequence.

Some Creatures, like this **Uni-Knight**, have abilities that require Actions to use. See how it says "Pay 1 Action >>>"? You need to spend one of your Actions to use this ability. You can even use this ability twice, for an additional Action.

You can also spend an Action to draw a card! Or use both of your Actions to draw two cards. This is a fine way to spend your Actions if your Landscapes are already full of Creatures and Buildings.

# Fighting

Okay, time to turn up the juice and get serious. Time to talk about fighting. We talk about fighting a lot, because fighting is the way you win Card Wars.

During your Fight phase, all your Creatures that are in the Ready position MUST Fight. You get to choose the order in which your Creatures Fight.

When you Activate a Creature to Fight, look at your opponent's side of the Lane. If they do not have a Creature on their side of the Lane, your Creature deals its Attack value to your opponent's Hit Points. Do this enough times, and you'll reach Cool Guy status in no time.

If there is a Creature on the other side of a Lane when a Creature Activates to Fight, both will deal Damage to each other. Each Creature deals Damage equal to its ATK value to the opposing Creature. Even though Flooped Creatures do not fight on your turn, they still have to Fight back if your opponent Attacks on their turn.

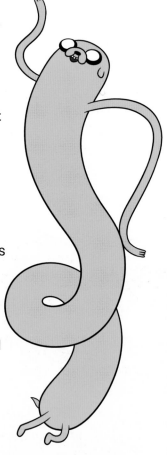

Damage does not carry over! If you use a Creature with 3 ATK to Fight a Creature with 1 DEF remaining, you will destroy your opponent's Creature, but it won't affect their Hit Points.

# ADVANCED STRATEGY:

## What Is Your Deck Trying to Do?

Yeah, I've been playing Card Wars for almost a thousand years, so leave it to me. I'll teach you some killer strategies to ensure you're always the Cool Guy and never the Dweeb.

The first time you flip through the cards in a Card Wars deck, you should try to figure out what the deck wants to *do*. What is the deck's goal? This is kind of a trick question, because the goal of every deck is to reduce your opponent's Hit Points to 0, but each deck has radically different strategies for achieving this goal.

Most decks rely on some form of synergy. For example, take a look at these three cards from BMO's Useless Swamp deck.

**Wandering Bald Man** does not seem like a very good card. He has ATK of 0, and normally his ability would be considered a downside. "At the start of your turn, put the top card of your deck into your discard pile." In reality, his DEF of 10 buys you time while his discard ability enables the rest of the deck to do its thing. Cards with effects like this are called **enablers**.

**Dark Angel** gets more powerful if you have a bunch of cards in your discard pile. See how this works now? Dark Angel is a **payoff** card for the strategy Wandering Bald Man enabled.

**Gray Eyebat** has an ability that allows you to return Useless Swamp Creatures from your discard pile to your hand. This ability gives you more control than paying 1 Action to draw a card from the top of your deck. It's a different kind of synergy from Dark Angel, but it's also fueled by Wandering Bald Man. It's part of a **combo**.

<Hello! I wanted to show you another synergy between some cards in my deck, Lady Rainicorn's SandyLands deck.>

<**Sandsnake** has an ATK of 0, but deals 4 Damage to the opposing Creature in its Lane when it enters play. Enablers like **Sand Sphinx** allow you to repeat this effect. Imagine you are facing down a powerful Creature like Immortal Maize Walker. You could play Sandsnake, deal 4 Damage to **Immortal Maize Walker**, Floop Sand Sphinx to return Sandsnake to your hand, and then replay Sandsnake, dealing another 4 Damage to the Maize Walker, sending it to the discard pile, without ever attacking! On your next turn, you can Floop Sand Sphinx and play Sandsnake again!>

Sandsnake

1

SandyLands Creature

When Sandsnake enters play, deal 4 Damage to target opposing Creature in this Lane.

0 ⚔

9

Sand Sphinx

...ands Building

...um a Creature you ...e to its owner's hand.

Immortal Maize Walker

Swamp Creature

...tal Maize Walker is ...d Landscape, it deals ...e Damage.

8

Hey, hero! Princess Bubblegum here to enlighten you on the delicate art of placing Creatures on Landscapes. It's a lot more complex than it looks, okay? So let me show you what I know!

Sometimes it can be difficult to choose where you want to place your Creature. Here are some questions to ask yourself to help you decide.

*   Will any of your Creatures go to the discard pile after they Attack this turn? If so, consider replacing them with new Creatures, so that you do not take additional Damage on your opponent's turn.

*   Are there any empty Lanes where you could sneak in Damage this turn if you play a Creature in that Lane?

*   How much Damage has each of your opponent's Creatures taken? If you play a Creature in the same Lane as one of theirs, can you send it to the discard pile this turn? What about on their next turn?

*   Do any of your cards or your opponent's cards have special effects that can be triggered by taking Damage, discarding, or drawing cards, Flooping, or other moves? Be aware and plan accordingly!

If you have a Creature in each Lane and none is in danger of going to the discard pile, don't feel like you *have* to replace one of your Creatures with a new one. You can always spend your Actions to play Spells or Buildings and draw cards instead. That said, with some decks, like Lumpy Space Princess's totally lumped-up deck, you might want to replace lots of Creatures early in the game.

The practice of looking at the placement of an opponent's Creatures and deciding where is best to deploy your Creatures is called **Evaluating the Game State**. It takes practice to get right, but you'll have a huge edge over your opponent if you can master this technique.

If you are ever in doubt of where to place a Creature, and there is a Lane where your opponent has a Creature and you do not, put your Creature in that Lane.

# Sequencing

Hey, dudes. Here's the truth. There's so much more to strategy in Card Wars than just summoning Creatures, casting Spells, and Flooping pigs.

**No there's not!**

Quiet, bud! If you want to become the Cool Guy, you need to learn about **sequencing**.

After you draw a card on your turn and before you Fight, you can do a bunch of things in any order. You can spend an Action to draw a card. You can play Creatures. You can play Spells. You can Floop Creatures. You can do these things in any order, but some orders are better than others!

No two game states are the same, so I can't tell you the exact right thing to do in every situation. You gotta use your noodle and figure it out by looking at the cards on the table. But there are some things to look for. Liiiiiiiike . . .

Let's say you have **The Pig** in one Lane and **Embarrassing Bard** next to it. You want to Floop both Creatures this turn. Which Creature do you Floop first? No-brainer, right? You Floop The Pig first. Why? Because if you Floop Embarrassing Bard first, you will draw one card, but if you Floop The Pig and then Floop Embarrassing Bard, you will draw two cards instead! You just drew an extra card FOR FREE because you sequenced your Floops properly.

Another good suggestion is to always draw cards first if you want to draw cards. So Floop those Creatures, play those Spells that draw cards, and if you want, spend Actions to draw cards *before* you use any Actions to play Creatures or Spells. How come? Well, what if you draw a Creature that is BETTER than the Creature you intended to play this turn? Wouldn't you rather play the new, awesome Creature than that old, crummy one? Heck yes!

This ties into another concept of strategy known as **Card Advantage**. The next page knows tons about that!

# Card Advantage

Still here? Yeesh! You must really have some time on your hands. Good thing I'm here to teach you something important about playing Card Wars. **Card Advantage!**

The key to playing well is making good choices. Cards are options, so the more cards, the better.

In defensive decks, like my Blue Plains deck, having more cards than your opponent is the key to victory.

Take a look at my **Embarrassing Bard** Creature. He has 1 ATK and 5 DEF. Not too impressive, but the Floop ability is what makes this dude shine. You'll draw *at least* an extra card every turn, without spending Actions. Sure, you won't Attack with the Embarrassing Bard after you Floop him, but that's okay. If your opponent has a Creature in the Bard's Lane, it will peck away at his DEF, but in the meantime you'll be drawing a buttload of free cards. To really go wild drawing cards, play **Cool Dog** in the Lane next to Embarrassing Bard. Cool Dog makes it super hard for your opponent's Creatures to Fight at all!

You better be careful, dude. Some cards punish you if you draw too many cards, like the super-diabolical **Field of Nightmares** Spell from my Cornfield deck.

Listen up, I'm going to teach you a cruel and unforgiving strategy that will make you the best Card Wars player in the Land of Ooo.

Let's say you have a **Nice Ice Baby** in your hand. Your opponent has a **Wall of Sand** on the board. It's your turn, and you want to play the Nice Ice Baby. But where should you put it? Hmm? I'll scratch my bushy white beard while you think.

If you play your Nice Ice Baby facing the Wall, it will go to the discard pile after just one or two hits. If you don't get in the way of the Wall of Sand, it will peck away at your Hit Points by 1 or 3 every turn. But who cares? If you play Nice Ice Baby in a Lane without a Creature, you'll deal 4 Damage per turn to your opponent's Hit Points.

So think about it! It doesn't matter if you only have 1 Hit Point left, as long as your opponent has 0 Hit Points left. It's okay to take some hits if it means you win! That's using your Hit Points as a resource.

# Jake's Cornfield Deck

My Cornfield deck is about corn! Corn, corn, corn! The more corn you have, the better! My deck is a hyper-aggressive rough-house that is at its most powerful when you have four Cornfield Landscapes. **Corn Ronin** and **Husker Knight** both pack a bigger punch if you have more Cornfield Landscapes. **Corn Lord** gets better if you control more Corn Creatures, and **Husker Worm** has 5 ATK. That's just crazy corn. Combine these aggressive Creatures with other Creatures and Spells that throw Damage right in your opponent's face when you play them, like **Corn Scepter** and **Cornataur**.

Your defensive Creatures also work better with more Cornfield Landscapes, making **Wall of Ears** a 2/8, **Corn Dog** a 0/16, and **Patchy the Pumpkin** (who should Floop every turn) deal Damage to every Creature your opponent has in play. Brutality! With this combo, it will be almost impossible for your opponent's Creatures to break through.

# Decklist

| Number in Deck | Name | Type | Landscape |
|---|---|---|---|
| 2 | Big Foot | Creature | Rainbow |
| 1 | Evil Eye | Creature | Rainbow |
| 1 | Phyllis | Creature | Rainbow |
| 1 | Drooling Dude | Creature | Rainbow |
| 2 | Travelin' Farmer | Creature | Cornfield |
| 1 | Corn Lord | Creature | Cornfield |
| 2 | Corn Ronin | Creature | Cornfield |
| 2 | Wall of Ears | Creature | Cornfield |
| 2 | Husker Worm | Creature | Cornfield |
| 2 | Patchy the Pumpkin | Creature | Cornfield |
| 2 | Field Stalker | Creature | Cornfield |
| 2 | Cornataur | Creature | Cornfield |
| 2 | Legion of Earlings | Creature | Cornfield |
| 2 | Husker Knight | Creature | Cornfield |
| 1 | Field Reaper | Creature | Cornfield |
| 1 | Corn Dog | Creature | Cornfield |
| 1 | Archer Dan | Creature | Cornfield |
| 2 | Field of Nightmares | Spell | Cornfield |
| 2 | Teleport | Spell | Rainbow |
| 2 | Reclaim Landscape | Spell | Rainbow |
| 2 | Corn Scepter | Spell | Rainbow |
| 1 | Cross Pollination | Spell | Rainbow |
| 1 | Silo of Truth | Building | Cornfield |
| 1 | Celestial Castle | Building | Rainbow |
| 2 | Blood Fortress | Building | Rainbow |

The most important enablers to my Cornfield deck are Cornfield Landscapes themselves. These Landscapes power up a bazillion of the Cornfield Creatures in my deck. And you don't even need to play them! They are there at the start of the game. Just don't get them flipped over by something like **The Pig** or **Volcano**, or you could lose a powerful effect at the worst possible moment.

Landscape

Cornfield

© 2013 Cryptozoic Entertainment   TM & © Cartoon Network (13)

Big Foot

Rainbow Creature

FLOOP »»» Flip target face-down Landscape you control face up.

**Big Foot** is a Rainbow Creature with a Floop ability that allows you to turn a facedown Landscape you control faceup. Your Cornfield Landscapes are essential to your strategy with this deck, and you need them faceup to succeed. This Creature will ensure that your Landscapes are always faceup.

The Rainbow Building **Blood Fortress** boosts your Creatures' Attack power.

Blood Fortress

Rainbow Building

Your Creature in this Lane has +1 ATK.

Use **Legion of Earlings** to return your opponent's Creature to their hand and then hit them for 2 in the face immediately.

Legion of Earlings

Cornfield Creature

When Legion of Earlings enters play, you may return target Creature in this Lane to its owner's hand.

**Husker Knight** is one of the nastiest Creatures in all of Card Wars. In my Cornfield deck it will usually have 4 ATK and 8 DEF. That's enough to wipe out many Creatures in one or two Fights. It's not uncommon for Husker Knight cards to trade for two, three, or even four of your opponent's cards. That's a whole lot of value. Just be careful—if your Husker Knight card has 6 Damage on it and one of your Landscapes gets flipped facedown, the Husker Knight will go to the discard pile on the spot!

**Patchy the Pumpkin** is incredibly powerful, and can carve up your opponent's Creatures with ease. Because Patchy can Floop every turn, it will take several turns for your opponent to Attack through it. Try to play Patchy in a Lane where your opponent has a Creature with 0 or 1 ATK to gain extra value.

Patchy the Pumpkin and **Corn Scepter** demonstrate the value of a card. Remember, you always want your cards to provide the biggest possible effect for the lowest cost. That's how you win over your opponent. Corn Scepter does 4 Damage on one turn. Patchy also does 4 Damage on one turn, spread out over four enemy Creatures. Then the next turn, Patchy does it again, and again, every turn. Then your opponent also has to get rid of Patchy, and that taxes their resources further. So you see, Patchy the Pumpkin is the better card in more situations because of the repeatable effect.

In addition to gaining value from Cornfield Landscapes, my deck has a secondary angle of Attack. Would you expect anything less from the military tactical genius of Jake the Dog? The secondary strategy is to punish your opponent for having lots of cards in their hands. **Field Stalker** makes each player draw an additional card on your turn. Normally it would be bad to give your opponent extra cards, but once you see the combos with this strategy, it will all make sense.

**Field of Nightmares** combos with effects like Field Stalker in a super-cool way. True, the extra card helps you, too, but it works best when you get to deal even more Damage to your opponent. The effect is even stronger against Finn's Blue Plains deck, which draws cards faster than most decks. Dealing a bunch of Damage directly to an opponent isn't a big deal early in the game when you are trying to get Creatures into play, but it is excellent when you're trying to get rid of your opponent's last few Hit Points. That said, if your opponent ends a turn with a bunch of cards in hand, don't be afraid to fire off one of these nasty Spells.

**Travelin' Farmer** has the same effect as Field of Nightmares, except he's a Creature. We already know why this effect is great. Remember, it doesn't matter how Travelin' Farmer leaves play, so if you replace him by putting a fresh Creature on his Landscape, he will still deal Damage all the same.

The key to improving my aggressive Cornfield deck is consistency. Try to get more copies of the strongest Corn Creatures and Spells like **Husker Knight**, **Patchy the Pumpkin**, and **Legion of Earlings**. Cards like **Ethan Allfire**, **Sun King**, and **Ring of Damage** from the For the Glory! Booster Pack will also help this aggressive strategy succeed. Remember, you can only have THREE copies of a card in your deck at a time.

Look for the **Yellow Lighthouse** Building and the rare **Quadurai** Rainbow Creature from the booster pack. These cards give your anti-card-draw strategy a boost. There are more ways to improve this strategy, but you will have to look beyond Cornfield Landscapes and add a second type. Check out the Rainbow section of this guide for more information.

It's up to you to decide what direction you want to take my groovy Cornfield deck. If you add a second Landscape type, your corn-powered Creatures will be weaker overall, so feel free to take some of them out. If you want to double down on corn, remove cards that don't support your all-out Attack strategy: **Cross Pollination**, **Corn Dog**, **Celestial Castle**.

# Finn's Blue Plains Deck

If you want to feel like a hero genius with boss card-drawing powers, then my Blue Plains deck is the deck for you. What's better than drawing cards? Drawing more cards! Ha-ha! My deck is what you'd call a *combo* deck. It will put your Card Wars skills to the ultimate test. It's not for the faint of heart, but if you know how to use it, you can crush any enemy. My deck combines card-draw effects like **Gnome Snot** and **Embarrassing Bard** with cheap Spells like **Teleport** and **Woad Talisman** so you can play lots of cards on a single turn. And my deck is full of Creatures that grow more powerful when you play Spells, change Lanes, or Floop. **Punk Cat** gives each Creature that changes Lanes a bonus, while **Woadic Chief** gets stronger every time you play a Spell. Then you use Floop abilities like the one on **Ancient Scholar** to get back your Spells and repeat the process all over again.

# Decklist

| Number in Deck | Name | Type | Landscape |
|---|---|---|---|
| 2 | The Pig | Creature | Rainbow |
| 2 | Nice Ice Baby | Creature | Rainbow |
| 2 | Dragon Claw | Creature | Blue Plains |
| 2 | Ancient Scholar | Creature | Blue Plains |
| 2 | Psionic Architect | Creature | Blue Plains |
| 2 | X-Large Spirit Soldier | Creature | Blue Plains |
| 1 | Uni-Knight | Creature | Blue Plains |
| 2 | Struzann Jinn | Creature | Blue Plains |
| 2 | Embarrassing Bard | Creature | Blue Plains |
| 1 | Woadic Chief | Creature | Blue Plains |
| 2 | Cool Dog | Creature | Blue Plains |
| 2 | Woadic Marauder | Creature | Blue Plains |
| 2 | Punk Cat | Creature | Blue Plains |
| 1 | Heavenly Gazer | Creature | Blue Plains |
| 1 | Woad Blood | Spell | Rainbow |
| 2 | Teleport | Spell | Rainbow |
| 2 | Woad Talisman | Spell | Rainbow |
| 2 | Cerebral Bloodstorm | Spell | Rainbow |
| 2 | Gnome Snot | Spell | Blue Plains |
| 2 | Woad Mobile Home | Building | Blue Plains |
| 1 | Schoolhouse | Building | Blue Plains |
| 2 | Celestial Castle | Building | Rainbow |
| 1 | Blood Fortress | Building | Rainbow |

Some Creatures in the deck get a bonus when you have Flooped Creatures. Other Creatures get a bonus when they change Lanes. **Dragon Claw** does both, so having it in play and Flooping every turn is a great way to get the Blue Plains deck's engine going. All aboard the combo train. Woo-woooooo!

Two of this deck's biggest problems are running out of Spells and running out of Actions. **Ancient Scholar** helps with both of those issues, and like Dragon Claw, it Floops as well.

**Embarrassing Bard** draws a card or two every turn, as long as you Floop him. The Bard is one of the best cards to help you gain card advantage.

Floop **Woad Mobile Home** every turn if you can.

With all the Floop Creatures in the Blue Plains deck, **Struzann Jinn** could potentially be a 7 ATK, 11 DEF Creature. That is one big dude. If you draw him early in the game, you can use him to get in the way of a powerful early attacker. If you draw him later, set up a game state where you have lots of Floop Creatures in play, so that Struzann Jinn can Attack for big chunks of Damage.

**Woadic Chief** is the Creature in the deck that gets the most benefit from playing a bunch of Spells. Imagine this sequence: Play a **Teleport** Spell to move Woadic Chief to a Lane where your opponent doesn't have a Creature. Then play two **Woad Talisman** Spells in a row. Now Woadic Chief has 12 Attack. That's nearly half your opponent's Hit Points.

**Woadic Marauder** helps replace cheap Spells.

**Punk Cat** gives bonuses when Creatures change Lanes.

# Finn's Blue Plains Deck
## Combos (Synergy)

The Blue Plains deck wants you to play a flurry of 0-Action Spells every turn, but you only get two copies of **Teleport** in your deck. **Ancient Scholar** is one way to get those Teleports back, and if you have a Building in the Scholar's Lane, you can gain precious Actions each turn as well.

**Nice Ice Baby** packs a big punch when it Fights unopposed in a Lane, but usually after one hit, your opponent will play a Creature to defend and you'll lose your precious Nice Ice Baby on the next Attack. **Dragon Claw** allows you to move the Baby to a new Lane where it can Attack freely with its bonus once more.

**Cool Dog** is a card that combos with itself! If you can place two Cool Dog cards next to each other in the middle two Lanes, you'll have complete protection for your Creatures in all four Lanes. Your opponent won't be able to Fight you at all! (Just remember that you still do have to Fight.)

# Finn's Blue Plains Deck
## Improvements

## From Lumpy Space Princess's
## Blue Plains/Useless Swamp Deck:

You gotta hand it to LSP, she has stashed some lumpy Blue Plains cards in her deck that can make Finn's Blue Plains deck fiercer than an ogre with a toothache. **Pants of Awesome** is a Spell with great utility because it teleports a Creature and draws a card. **Travelin' Skeleton** can give you a Lane change bonus when you have a Creature in each of the four Lanes—no easy feat. **Subliminal Strength** can be a great finisher to a chain of cheap Spells, making your dudes Attack for massive Damage, while **Strength Crystal** refills your hand and keeps the cheap Spells coming.

## From Elsewhere:

You can beef up your deck with more Creatures that care about the things the Blue Plains deck wants to do. **Blue Ogre** and **Paladim** both fit the bill. **Spell Warp** can give Lane change bonuses to two Creatures on the same turn, while **Puma Paw** lets your Floopable Creatures use their abilities while keeping them ready to Fight (or Floop again). **Igloo of Sanctuary** provides one of the biggest bonuses to a Creature that changes Lanes. You should also max out your copies of your best cards like **Teleport**, **Woad Talisman**, **Punk Cat**, and others. Keep an eye on Creatures that cost 1 Action to play. The default list for this deck has too many 2-Action Creatures to compete with aggressive decks.

# BMO's Useless Swamp Deck

Hello, friend! It is me, BMO! Who wants to play Card Wars? Although I do not play such games with Jake, I am happy to play with you! My deck is the best. It is the Useless Swamp deck from the BMO vs. Lady Rainicorn Collector's Pack. It makes my circuits warm just thinking about it. You see, the deck focuses on the discard pile, a place where trash goes. But these cards are not trash to me! They are . . . *my babies*.

My Useless Swamp deck uses Spells, Creatures, and Floop abilities to put cards into my discard pile. Many of my Spells and Creatures get stronger if I have 5, 10, 15, or more cards in my discard pile. Early in the game, I like to play strong defensive Creatures like **Wandering Bald Man** and **Chest Burster** to keep my opponent's Creatures from frying my circuits, then focus on filling up my discard pile. Once my discard pile is big enough, I turn into a supercomputer, capable of defeating my opponents with Creatures that are oh-so-strong (but I defeat them nicely, I promise). If I ever discard a useful card, don't cry—I can use the abilities on **Gray Eyebat** and **Tree of Undeath** to retrieve and replay Creatures over and over again. My Useless Swamp deck is anything but useless!

# Decklist

| Number in Deck | Name | Type | Landscape |
|---|---|---|---|
| 2 | Wandering Bald Man | Creature | Rainbow |
| 2 | Gray Eyebat | Creature | Useless Swamp |
| 2 | Chest Burster | Creature | Useless Swamp |
| 2 | Hot Eyebat | Creature | Useless Swamp |
| 2 | Mouthball | Creature | Useless Swamp |
| 2 | Red Eyeling | Creature | Useless Swamp |
| 2 | Extraordinary Spider | Creature | Useless Swamp |
| 2 | Mace Stump | Creature | Useless Swamp |
| 2 | Green Mermaid | Creature | Useless Swamp |
| 1 | Dark Angel | Creature | Useless Swamp |
| 1 | Tree of Undeath | Creature | Useless Swamp |
| 1 | Green Merman | Creature | Useless Swamp |
| 1 | Teeth Leaf | Creature | Useless Swamp |
| 1 | Dr. Death | Creature | Useless Swamp |
| 2 | Immortal Maize Walker | Creature | Useless Swamp |
| 1 | Blonde MerWitch | Creature | Rainbow |
| 2 | Bone Wand | Spell | Rainbow |
| 2 | Ogre Gas | Spell | Rainbow |
| 2 | Snake Eye Ring | Spell | Rainbow |
| 1 | Abraca Amadeus | Spell | Useless Swamp |
| 2 | Magic Ring Ding | Spell | Useless Swamp |
| 1 | Celestial Castle | Building | Rainbow |
| 2 | Blood Fortress | Building | Rainbow |
| 1 | Palace of Bone | Building | Useless Swamp |
| 1 | Spirit Tower | Building | Useless Swamp |

**Wandering Bald Man**

Rainbow Creature

At the start of your turn, put the top card of your deck into your discard pile.

0 ⚡          ⬡10

**Wandering Bald Man** is a cheap early blocker and a great way to start adding cards to your discard pile. Even if his time in play is brief, Wandering Bald Man will have a strong impact on the game.

**Ogre Gas** is a very misleading Spell. At first glance it looks like Ogre Gas doesn't do anything, but in fact it gives you card selection and an interesting combo. First, think of it as saying, "Discard the top 2 cards of your library." Not great, but a decent effect when so many of your cards care about having a bunch of cards in the discard pile. Also, remember that a number of cards in BMO's Useless Swamp deck can return Creatures and Spells from your discard pile to your hand.

**Ogre Gas**

Rainbow Spell

Reveal the top 3 cards of your deck. Put one of them on the bottom of your deck and discard the rest.

**Green Merman**

Useless Swamp Creature

FLOOP >>> Put the top card of your deck into your discard pile. Deal damage to each opposing Creature equal to the discarded card's Action Cost.

0 ⚡          ⬡ 6

**Green Merman** lets you put a card into your discard pile every turn, and can do big Damage to all your opponent's Creatures at the same time.

# BMO's Useless Swamp Deck
## Payoffs

Once you have a stack of 5 discards, **Extraordinary Spider** will deal Damage to your opponent every turn, regardless of whether or not your opponent has a Creature in the Spider's Lane. If you have 10 or 15 cards in your discard pile, Extraordinary Spider will win the game for you after enough turns, and it is even more threatening in multiples.

In a deck that discards often, **Tree of Undeath**'s ability basically reads, "Floop >>> Draw a card." You can also create a loop where you are replacing damaged Creatures with fresh ones, and then Flooping back the replaced ones to your hand with this ability.

**Gray Eyebat** gains value if you have Creatures in your discard pile. Remember, you can always pay 1 Action to draw the top card of your deck, so before you use Gray Eyebat's ability, look through your discard pile and make sure the card you're getting back is better than a random unknown card.

**Hot Eyebat** is difficult to play early in the game, but nothing compares to its efficiency. 4 ATK is a crazy-good ability.

Don't let his vegetarian physique fool you; **Teeth Leaf** has a beefy body—and playing him for free feels *real* nice.

# BMO's Useless Swamp Deck
## Combos

**Red Eyeling** combos with a lot of different cards, making it one of the strongest in Card Wars. **Bone Wand** is a great one because you can repeatedly force your opponent to discard a card. You can even do it twice in one turn. Once your opponent's hand is empty, they will have a hard time keeping up, as they will have to spend Actions to draw cards instead of playing Creatures. Then when it's your turn, you can easily force your opponent to discard the cards they just drew.

This combo of **Abraca Amadeus** and **Chest Burster** represents another strategy for BMO's Useless Swamp deck. Force your opponent to discard their whole hand and then punish them for it.

# BMO's Useless Swamp Deck
## Improvements

The discard theme of my Useless Swamp deck goes in a couple of different directions. To improve the deck, you have to choose which strategy you prefer, and then adjust the list to better suit that strategy. Here are some helpful suggestions!

## Self-Discard

**Blue Merlock** allows you to sculpt your hand and discard cards you don't need (or cards you can easily retrieve with other Floop abilities). You can also discard powerful 2-Action Creatures and then use **Raise the Dead** to put them directly into play at a discount. Once your discard pile fills up, you can use **Fright Tower** to boost your Creatures' ATK, and **Cardboard Mansion** to play more Actions every turn.

## Opponent Discard

**Black Paladin** does an unholy job of smashing your opponent's face after you make them discard a bunch of cards. Wham! **Lt. Mushroom** can really rip your opponent's hand apart, but you have to play the card at the right time against the right Creature. **Smoldering Elder** has a similar effect that is easier to control.

# Lady Rainicorn's SandyLands Deck

< SandyLands Creatures are known for their powerful effects when they enter play. My SandyLands deck from the BMO vs. Lady Rainicorn Collector's Pack takes advantage of these Creatures by surrounding them with Spells and Floop abilities that return those Creatures to your hand.

SandyLands is an aggressive deck that can stick it out in the long game by returning and replaying Creatures before they get sent to the discard pile. **Sandsnake** is especially dangerous. It can wallop one of your opponent's high DEF Creatures by returning and replaying two or three times in a single turn. And with 9 DEF, Sandsnake can usually hold its own until the following turn when it can be returned again. If you like to float like a rainicorn and sting like a bouncy bee, do the SandyLands dance with my SandyLands deck. >

**1** Sandsnake

**SandyLands Creature**

When Sandsnake enters play, deal 4 Damage to target opposing Creature in this Lane.

**0** **9**

# Decklist

| Number in Deck | Name | Type | Landscape |
|---|---|---|---|
| 2 | Sand Angel | Creature | Rainbow |
| 1 | Ms. Mummy | Creature | Rainbow |
| 2 | Peach Djinni | Creature | Rainbow |
| 1 | Fummy | Creature | SandyLands |
| 1 | Sand Knight | Creature | SandyLands |
| 2 | Beach Mummy | Creature | SandyLands |
| 2 | Sandhorn Devil | Creature | SandyLands |
| 2 | SandWitch | Creature | SandyLands |
| 2 | Sandsnake | Creature | SandyLands |
| 2 | Green Cactiball | Creature | SandyLands |
| 2 | Shark | Creature | SandyLands |
| 2 | Wall of Sand | Creature | SandyLands |
| 2 | Sand Eyebat | Creature | SandyLands |
| 2 | The Mariachi | Creature | SandyLands |
| 1 | Lost Golem | Creature | SandyLands |
| 2 | Teleport | Spell | Rainbow |
| 2 | Unempty Coffin | Spell | Rainbow |
| 2 | ZaZo's Magic Seeds | Spell | Rainbow |
| 1 | Tome of Ankhs | Spell | SandyLands |
| 2 | Cerebral Bloodstorm | Spell | Rainbow |
| 1 | Celestial Castle | Building | Rainbow |
| 2 | Blood Fortress | Building | Rainbow |
| 2 | Sand Sphinx | Building | SandyLands |

**Fummy** is good. It might even be too good. Every player is always starved for Actions. More Actions can draw more cards, play more Spells, and play more Creatures. Getting an extra Action just because you have Fummy in play is crazy. Protect Fummy at all costs, and you'll race ahead of your opponent in no time.

**Sand Sphinx** and **Beach Mummy** are the cards that make the deck go 'round, each able to return a Creature to your hand every turn. Sand Sphinx doesn't take up a Landscape and can't be destroyed in a Fight, so even though it costs 2 Actions to

play, once you've put it into play, it will keep on giving. Beach Mummy is more flexible and cheaper to play, but you'll have to perfect your evasive maneuvers to keep it in play.

**Unempty Coffin** lets you put any creature on the board for free.

# Lady Rainicorn's SandyLands Deck Payoffs

When you start playing combos, returning and replaying Creatures and returning them again all on the same turn, cards like **SandWitch** can kick sand at your opponent's Hit Points. If you have a strong enough engine going, SandWitch can be a win condition, but it isn't the strongest payoff card in the deck.

Returning Creatures to your hand ensures that you'll have more Creatures to play, allowing you to set up strong Attacks with this 0-Action Spell. **ZaZo's Magic Seeds** should plant the idea in your head that playing and replaying Creatures, and then getting bonuses from Spells like this, is a strategy that will bear fruit.

**The Mariachi** can use his Floop ability to finish off your opponent's Creatures so that your own fighters don't have to get messed up in combat.

It's a safe bet that once **Wall of Sand** hits a Landscape, he'll be sticking around awhile. Remember: Wall of Sand is a SandyLand Creature, and counts toward his own ability.

# Lady Rainicorn's SandyLands Deck Combos

**Lost Golem** is a super powerful Creature, but difficult to play from your hand. Here's one sequence that squeezes a lot of extra juice out of your hand. Let's say you have Lost Golem, **Peach Djinni, Fummy,** and **Shark** in hand. **Sand Sphinx** is in play. First, play Peach Djinni; 2 Actions left. Play Fummy in the Lane with Sand Sphinx. Peach Djinni gets +1 ATK; 1 Action left. Floop Fummy; 2 Actions left. Floop Sand Sphinx, returning Fummy to your hand; 2 Actions left. Play Fummy. Peach Djinni gets +1 ATK; 1 Action left. Floop Fummy; 2 Actions left. Play Shark. Shark gets +1 ATK. Peach Djinni gets +1 ATK; 0 Actions left. Play Lost Golem for 0 Actions because of the 4 Creatures you have already played this turn. Shark gives Lost Golem +1 ATK. Peach Djinni gets +1 ATK. Did you follow all of that? Now you Fight, dealing a total of 13 DAMAGE to your opponent! Now here is a quiz: Can you think of a sequence with these cards that gives you an even better result?

**Psychic Tempest**

SandyLands Spell

Return all Creatures in play you own to your hand. *(This includes stolen Creatures.)*

**Portal of Unsummoning**

SandyLands Spell

Return target Creature to its owner's hand.

**Sand Pyramid**

SandyLands Building

Pay 2 Actions >>> Return each Creature in this Lane to its owner's hand. *(Affects both players.)*

**Temple of the Sun**

SandyLands Building

When a SandyLands Creature with cost 1 or greater you control enters play in this Lane, you may return it to its owner's hand.

In terms of Spells and Buildings, there are quality choices that can throw your return-a-Creature strategy into overdrive. **Psychic Tempest** will reset your Landscapes, returning to your hand all the Creatures you have in play. **Portal of Unsummoning** can return *any* Creature, including an opponent's Creature. That can undo your foe's entire turn, and allow you to hit your opponent without obstruction. **Sand Pyramid** and **Temple of the Sun** are two SandyLands Buildings that return Creatures to hand and are great additions to the deck.

**Green Party Ogre**

SandyLands Creature

When a Creature you control leaves play, heal 1 Damage from Green Party Ogre.

1 / 8

**Green Snakey**

SandyLands Creature

When Green Snakey leaves play, deal 1 Damage to target Creature in this Lane.

1 / 6

**Lady Beetle**

SandyLands Creature

At the start of your turn, you may return a Creature you control with 2 or fewer DEF remaining to its owner's hand.

1 / 9

**Sandasaurus Rex**

SandyLands Creature

+2 ATK for each of your empty Landscapes.

0 / 9

**Ms. Mummy**

Rainbow Creature

At the start of your turn, you may return Ms. Mummy to its owner's hand. If you do, target SandyLand Creature you control gains 1 DEF.

1 / 4

There are a bunch of Creatures out in the wild you can add to Lady Rainicorn's SandyLands deck that fit perfectly with the strategy of returning Creatures to your hand. **Green Party Ogre** and **Green Snakey** give little benefits with each return. **Lady Beetle** returns your Creatures automatically if they are low on DEF. **Sandasaurus Rex** takes advantage of the fact that all the returns leave empty Lanes on your side, and **Ms. Mummy** is a great way to get a free return each turn without spending any Actions.

# Princess Bubblegum's NiceLands Deck

Hello, dear friends! Princess Bubblegum here to inform you of the loveliest of Card Wars decks, my NiceLands deck from the Princess Bubblegum vs. Lumpy Space Princess Collector's Pack. My deck contains a number of fluffy, delicious Creatures who, like me, are super polite. But if they get hurt, you'd better watch out! If these Creatures have a certain amount of Damage on them, their ATK goes through the gingerbread roof! The goal is to keep your Hit Points high until you get your Creatures to that point. You can accelerate this process with a number of sweet effects. **Cutie** can Floop to heal 1 Hit Point, and **Snakemint** heals Hit Points every time it deals Damage to an opponent. You can stall your opponent's Attack with **Cave of Solitude**. Once your Creatures reach the correct amount of Damage, you can use healing effects like **Blue Candy** and **Green Candy** to keep them there. The deck is a blast to play, and I hope you will be courteous to your opponent while dueling—until you power up your Creatures' ATK, then I hope you punch your enemy in the head!

# Decklist

| Number in Deck | Name | Type | Landscape |
|---|---|---|---|
| 2 | Cow | Creature | Rainbow |
| 2 | Angel Heart | Creature | Rainbow |
| 2 | Albino Eyebat | Creature | NiceLands |
| 2 | Cotton Eyebat | Creature | NiceLands |
| 2 | Wall of Chocolate | Creature | NiceLands |
| 1 | Ms. Fluff | Creature | NiceLands |
| 2 | Cutie | Creature | NiceLands |
| 2 | Apple Pieclops | Creature | NiceLands |
| 2 | Niceasaurus Rex | Creature | NiceLands |
| 2 | Rainbow Eyebat | Creature | NiceLands |
| 1 | Fairy Shepard | Creature | NiceLands |
| 2 | Pieclops | Creature | NiceLands |
| 2 | Angel of Vanilla | Creature | NiceLands |
| 1 | Angel of Chocolate | Creature | NiceLands |
| 2 | Snakemint | Creature | NiceLands |
| 2 | Ring of Fluffy | Spell | NiceLands |
| 1 | Falling Star | Spell | NiceLands |
| 2 | Piestorm | Spell | NiceLands |
| 2 | Blue Candy | Spell | NiceLands |
| 2 | Green Candy | Spell | Rainbow |
| 1 | Celestial Castle | Building | Rainbow |
| 1 | Blood Fortress | Building | Rainbow |
| 1 | Cave of Solitude | Building | NiceLands |
| 1 | Windmill of Health | Building | NiceLands |

Using **Apple Pieclops** requires forward thinking on your part. You have to calculate how much Damage will be dealt to your Creatures when you Fight on your turn, but also how hard your opponent will hit when they Fight. Usually, Apple Pieclops will buy you time and give your Creatures an edge over the enemy as you heal them all to keep them alive. But you can also use the deal Damage effect to increase the ATK of a Creature who works best with a specific amount of Damage. Those bonuses are how the NiceLands deck wins, so try to put the ability into effect whenever you can.

**Falling Star** is best played when you have Creatures in play with their ATK bonus abilities in effect. The Spell will ensure that you get two big hits with your Creatures, instead of just one, before they are damaged and lose the bonus. You can also use Falling Star if your Creatures will be sent to the discard pile after they Fight on your turn. That will keep them around through your opponent's Fight, meaning that when they are destroyed, you can play fresh Creatures into empty Landscapes on your turn.

**Green Candy** is a ninja in your deck. It can tweak the amount of Damage on one of your Creatures to engage its ATK bonus, or it can pick off one of your opponent's damaged Creatures and spare you a Fight.

This pair of pale Eyebats is the skeleton of the NiceLands deck. Cheap to play, these cards come down easily and Fight just fine. They give you a nice ATK boost when you hit the magic number. **Albino Eyebat** is the more consistent of the two, but **Cotton Eyebat** has a higher payoff, and is probably the stronger Creature in this case.

**Albino Eyebat**

**1**

NiceLands Creature

While Albino Eyebat has exactly 2 Damage on it, it has +2 ATK.

**2** ⚔ · ♥ **7**

**Cotton Eyebat**

**1**

NiceLands Creature

While Cotton Eyebat has exactly 4 Damage on it, it has +4 ATK.

**1** ⚔ · ♥ **8**

**Ms. Fluff**

**2**

NiceLands Creature

While Ms. Fluff has exactly 7 Damage on it, it has +7 ATK.

**2** ⚔ · ♥ **10**

**Ms. Fluff** is queen of the NiceLands Creatures. It's not easy to get to exactly 7 Damage, but creating a 9 ATK Creature, if timed right, will often win a game on the spot. If you can combine Ms. Fluff with healing effects to get in multiple hits with her bonus active, you deserve a fluffy trophy.

In a deck without a lot of ways to draw cards, **Niceasaurus Rex** gets the job done.

**Niceasaurus Rex**

**1**

NiceLands Creature

At the start of your turn, if Niceasaurus Rex has Damage on it, draw a card.

**2** ⚔ · ♥ **7**

**Wall Of Chocolate**

**2**

NiceLands Creature

While Wall of Chocolate has no Damage on it, it has +3 ATK.

**1** ⚔ · ♥ **9**

**Wall of Chocolate** should be used primarily as a killer of utility Creatures.

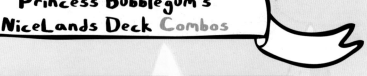

Both **Angel of Vanilla** and **Angel of Chocolate** have the ability to heal all Damage on them. Combine this ability every turn with the ATK bonus **Windmill of Health** gives to undamaged Creatures, and you will have a powerful, potent attacker that your opponent must deal with, because left alone, it is almost impossible to destroy.

**Piestorm** only costs 1 Action to play, so it combos aggressively with any other 1-Action Creature in the deck, but if you have a couple 0-Action Creatures like your trusty **Cow** in hand, you can really go to town by playing them all out on an early turn and then playing Piestorm to give all your fresh Creatures a boost. This allows you to get in against your opponent's Creatures, or even smack your opponent's Hit Points hard in the face. Later in the game, you can combine Piestorm with a healing spell like **Blue Candy** to ambush an opponent with a big hit.

There are a number of strong Creatures that will boost Bubblegum's Damage-management strategy in Marceline's NiceLands/Useless Swamp deck from the Ice King vs. Marceline Collector's Pack, including **Papercut Tiger** and **Furious Hen**. Marceline's deck also contains powerful Floop Creatures that will do good work for you, including **Dr. Stuffenstein**, who can help enable your ATK bonus Creatures, and **Cottonpult**, which does a great job of hurting your opponent's Creatures.

The For the Glory! Booster Pack also contains some powerful additions, including **Sack of Pain**, one of the best Creatures out there, which gets a whopping +6 ATK when it has 6 Damage on it, and the Rainbow Building **Fountain of Tears**, which gives the Damage-boost ability to any Creature in that Lane. (Remember, a Creature with the Damage-boost ability can also get the Fountain's ability.) **Nice Windmill** is a NiceLands Building that makes it easy to get your Creatures to the sweet spot, and **Master of Disguise** can blunt your enemy's ATK for a turn, allowing you to get in an extra hit with the bonus ATK if you time it right.

# Lumpy Space Princess's Blue Plains/Useless Swamp Deck

Oh, yeah, *finally* . . . we get to talk about my lumped-up deck from the Princess Bubblegum vs. Lumpy Space Princess Collector's Pack. It's totally hot. My deck is twice as good as everyone else's, because it uses two types of Landscapes—Blue Plains and Useless Swamp. It's, like, awesome.

When you're kicking butt with my deck, you're gonna be discarding like there's no mañana, and replacing Creatures, too. *Replacing* is when you play a Creature on a Landscape where another Creature is already chillin', doing his thang, and then, wham! You play another Creature and the older Creature goes buh-bye, all the way to the discard pile. It's pretty cutthroat, but so's life. So get used to it, girl!

If you think my deck is weird, then whatever! I'm not, like, gonna cry or anything. Besides, my Blue Plains cards are sweet in any Blue Plains deck, and my Useless Swamp cards are awesome in any Useless Swamp deck. Those decks *need* me. And I'm, like, the most charitable princess I *know*, so I'm happy to spread the wealth.

# Decklist

| Number in Deck | Name | Type | Landscape |
|---|---|---|---|
| 2 | Goat | Creature | Rainbow |
| 2 | Brain Gooey | Creature | Blue Plains |
| 2 | Grape Djini | Creature | Blue Plains |
| 2 | Blueberry Djini | Creature | Blue Plains |
| 2 | Future Scholar | Creature | Blue Plains |
| 1 | Headphone Jerk | Creature | Blue Plains |
| 1 | Travelin' Skeleton | Creature | Blue Plains |
| 2 | Dragon Foot | Creature | Useless Swamp |
| 2 | Dogboy | Creature | Rainbow |
| 2 | Herculeye | Creature | Useless Swamp |
| 1 | Pink Merwitch | Creature | Useless Swamp |
| 2 | Fatapillar | Creature | Useless Swamp |
| 1 | Skeletal Hand | Creature | Useless Swamp |
| 2 | Steakchop | Creature | Useless Swamp |
| 1 | Volcano | Spell | Rainbow |
| 2 | Brief Power | Spell | Rainbow |
| 1 | Toilet of Doom | Spell | Useless Swamp |
| 1 | Mausoleum | Building | Useless Swamp |
| 1 | Night Tower | Building | Useless Swamp |
| 1 | Strength Crystal | Spell | Blue Plains |
| 1 | Pants of Awesome | Spell | Blue Plains |
| 2 | Subliminal Strength | Spell | Blue Plains |
| 1 | Pyramidia | Building | Blue Plains |
| 1 | Blood Fortress | Building | Rainbow |
| 2 | Squatting Bald Man | Creature | Useless Swamp |
| 2 | Infinite Figure | Creature | Useless Swamp |

**Skeletal Hand** has two main purposes in LSP's lumpy deck. First, it keeps you and your opponent at parity. *Parity* means you're about even in the game, in terms of cards, Hit Points, and Creatures in play. As you replace your Creatures with others, you may experience card *disadvantage*, because you won't be getting full value out of your Creatures. Skeletal Hand's ability, which makes your opponent discard cards, will reduce their hand size and allow you to keep pace. Skeletal Hand's other purpose is to fill up your discard pile, which hooks up some of the cards in the payoff section.

**Steakchop** is a massive attacker but hard to keep around. Discarding two cards a turn is too many to sustain over a long period. You can treat Steakchop as a one-shot attacker that you hit with once, get hit once, and then destroy it instead of discarding two cards. Often, however, you will need more cards in your discard pile, in which case, paying the cost is fine.

With all this discarding, you're going to need some way to refill your hand. **Strength Crystal** is the ticket.

**Herculeye** has a massive ATK and puts cards in your discard pile.

You will be familiar with payoff cards like **Fatapillar** from BMO's Useless Swamp deck. Put a bunch of cards in your discard pile and then Fatapillar gets superstrong. Be careful, though— with only 3 DEF, Fatapillar won't last long once you play him.

**Goat** is one of the more basic examples of a replacement bonus, but he helps to illustrate this type of Creature's value. Play him on a Creature that is about to be destroyed, draw a card, and you'll still have 2 Actions to play other Creatures and Spells.

It's always best to use **Headphone Jerk** when you know that you will destroy your opponent's Creature in the Lane where you play him.

The **Pyramidia** Building makes your replacement Creatures even better, and it combos awesomely with **Future Scholar**. If you have a Creature in the Lane with Pyramidia, you can Floop Pyramidia, play Future Scholar, and still have 2 Actions, as if you had played Future Scholar for free. Consider this play when sequencing your turns, and then you can really combo hard.

**Blueberry Djini** and **Grape Djini** play well together. Imagine you play Blueberry Djini, replacing a Creature. You draw 2 cards. Then you play Grape Djini, replacing Blueberry Djini, and you use Grape Djini's ability to put Blueberry Djini back on top of your deck. Then you draw Blueberry Djini and replace Grape Djini and draw another 2 cards. Yay, cards! Cards are yummy.

The first thing to consider when improving LSP's deck is what the deck is missing. The deck struggles to maintain card advantage while matching up Creature for Creature with a deck like Princess Bubblegum's.

A cheap card-draw spell like **Gnome Snot** can get the mucus flowing, while **Tree of Undeath** and **Elf Hut** get more cards into your hand. **Green Merman** gets cards into your discard pile while weakening your opponent's Creatures, and if you want to focus on your discard strategy, **Mace Stump** brings the pain.

Marceline's deck has a number of good replacement Creatures, including **Bog Bum** and **Bog Frog Bomb**.

If you want to get more aggressive, **Fisher Fish** hits your opponent directly if you play it on a Blue Plains Landscape (luckily you have those) and **Black Paladin** will reward you every turn you discard cards for various on-board effects. The key with LSP's deck is to choose one of the deck's angles of Attack and enhance it as much as you can. If you want to dramatically transform the deck, look to the Rainbow section on Blue Plains/Useless Swamp decks for ideas.

# Ice King's IcyLands Deck

Well . . . if it isn't those rascals I don't like very much at all. If you're talking to little old Ice King, then you must be here to learn about my IcyLands deck from the Ice King vs. Marceline Collector's Pack. The IcyLands deck is chock full of Spells and effects like **Snow Business** and **Snow Way** that put Frozen Tokens on your opponent's Landscapes, which is my way of saying, "Chill out!" Frozen Tokens keep your opponent from playing Creatures on those Landscapes, and they have to discard a card to remove the Frozen Token. Your deck gives you a bunch of benefits for having Frozen Tokens through Creatures like **Boarder Collie** and **Emperor Penguin** and Buildings like **Ice-olation Cell** and **Crystal Palace**. As for winning, it's easy with my cool IcyLands deck. There are a bunch of super-aggressive Creatures like **Spike Icicle** and **Snow Bunny** that will drop your opponent's Hit Points fast. You're definitely going to win lots of games of Card Wars with my IcyLands deck, and then you'll pick up lots of cool babes, and then you'll marry a bunch of beautiful princesses, and then you'll take over the world!

# Decklist

| Number in Deck | Name | Type | Landscape |
|---|---|---|---|
| 2 | Nice Ice Baby | Creature | Rainbow |
| 2 | Spike Icicle | Creature | Rainbow |
| 2 | Cold Soldier | Creature | IcyLands |
| 2 | Abdominal Snowman | Creature | IcyLands |
| 2 | Icemeister | Creature | IcyLands |
| 1 | Sprucy Lucy | Creature | IcyLands |
| 2 | Reign Deer | Creature | IcyLands |
| 2 | Frost Dragon | Creature | IcyLands |
| 2 | Slay Rider | Creature | IcyLands |
| 2 | Frozen Fish | Creature | IcyLands |
| 1 | Snow Angel | Creature | IcyLands |
| 2 | Emperor Penguin | Creature | IcyLands |
| 2 | Snow Bunny | Creature | IcyLands |
| 2 | Snow Dog | Creature | IcyLands |
| 1 | Boarder Collie | Creature | IcyLands |
| 2 | Frosty Frolic | Spell | IcyLands |
| 1 | Snow Way | Spell | IcyLands |
| 2 | Freeze Ray | Spell | IcyLands |
| 2 | Freezing Point | Spell | IcyLands |
| 2 | Frozen Heart | Spell | Rainbow |
| 1 | Celestial Castle | Building | Rainbow |
| 1 | Ice-olation Cell | Building | IcyLands |
| 1 | Snow Business | Building | IcyLands |
| 1 | Crystal Palace | Building | IcyLands |

**Freeze Ray** is your basic Freeze-a-Landscape Spell. It's best used in a Lane where you already have a Creature and your opponent does not. The text "draw a card" is the most important on this card, because Freeze Ray replaces itself, and your opponent will have to discard a card to remove the token, and they will not get that card back.

**Frost Dragon** is a good early play, but don't go freezing Landscapes willy-nilly before you have more Creatures in play. Once you're in control, you can start using Frost Dragon's ability to trigger your other effects that benefit from freezing Landscapes.

**Frozen Fish** will Freeze a Landscape automatically when you deal Damage to a Creature.

**Sprucy Lucy** is a decent Creature on her own, but really shines if you have a couple of Frozen Tokens dotting your opponent's side of the table. With a maximum of 6 ATK, Sprucy Lucy can be one killer conifer.

Sprucy Lucy

2

IcyLands Creature

Sprucy Lucy has +1 ATK for each Landscape with a Frozen token on it players control.

2 ⚔ 9

Abdominal Snowman

1

IcyLands Creature

+3 ATK while your opponent does not control a Creature in this Lane.

3 ⚔ 2

Check out the six-pack of cola on this guy! **Abdominal Snowman** is exactly the kind of cheap, aggressive Creature the IcyLands deck needs in order to take advantage of your opponent's hindered ability to play Creatures. Some people call Creatures like this *glass cannons*, because they are very strong but very fragile. You definitely want to play him in a Lane where your opponent has a Frozen Token and no Creature, to maximize his Damage-dealing potential.

Once your opponent's Landscapes are Frozen, play **Icemeister** and watch as the frostbite chews up the bad guys.

Icemeister

2

IcyLands Creature

At the start of your turn, deal 1 Damage to each Creature on a Landscape with a Frozen token on it.

1 ⚔ 10

Frosty Frolic

2

IcyLands Spell

Target player discards 1 card from her hand for each Landscape with a Frozen token on it she controls.

**Frosty Frolic** is the nightmare scenario for an opponent whose Landscapes have been frozen.

# Ice King's IcyLands Deck
## Combos

Snow Bunny has a high ATK but a low DEF, which means you want to play it across from an empty Lane, because it will get destroyed pretty quickly once your opponent puts something in its way. If you know your Snow Bunny is about to go bye-bye, you can destroy it yourself, Freeze an empty Landscape, and drop a Nice Ice Baby across from it. That way you can keep the pressure up.

There is a very *cool* two-turn combo with these two 2-Action cards. Play Reign Deer on the first turn. Be careful of Reign Deer's low DEF. You can Floop Reign Deer for no cards the turn you play it if it will keep him alive until your next turn. On your next turn, play Freezing Point to Freeze all your opponent's Landscapes. Then you can Floop Reign Deer to draw 4 cards—one for each Frozen Landscape. Don't play Freezing Point before Reign Deer because your opponent will likely spend their next turn removing some of your tokens.

The first step to making the IcyLands deck great is to max out some of your cheapest and hardest-hitting cards like **Spike Icicle** and **Nice Ice Baby.** You can find some great enhancements to the Ice King's deck in Gunter's deck. Try **Icy Intruder**—it's an easy way to keep your opponent's Landscapes Frozen. He pairs well with **Icy Commando**, which gains ATK from Frozen Landscapes. The **Floating Ice Palace** Building is another good pick that benefits from Frozen Landscapes—and Buildings are harder for your opponent to destroy!

There are also plenty of Rainbow cards that can strengthen your deck. **Ring of Damage** is a good one for pushing through, well, Damage! **Blood Fortress** is a Building that serves the same purpose. **Teleport** lets you move your Creatures to Lanes where your opponents have no Creatures—an essential strategy move for Ice King. **Unempty Coffin** is always useful for getting a lot of Creatures on the board at once, and **Snowvalanche** can really pummel your opponent's Frozen Landscapes. Check the Rainbow section for more ideas.

# Marceline's NiceLands/ Useless Swamp Deck

Prepare yourself, mortals, to behold the greatest Card Wars deck of all: my NiceLands/ Useless Swamp deck, or Nice/Swamp deck, from the Ice King vs. Marceline Collector's Pack. Mwahahaha! It is wicked, and I know you'll just love it. My deck has two goals, one for each of my fangs. First, it makes your opponent discard cards, then punishes your opponent for discarding cards. Heehee! The second thing my deck does is give its own Creatures a little tickle, and by "little tickle," I mean DAMAGE! The Creatures in my deck get stronger when they are damaged—some so strong, they can take out your opponent's Creatures in a single hit.

# Decklist

| Number in Deck | Name | Type | Landscape |
|---|---|---|---|
| 2 | Furious Chick | Creature | NiceLands |
| 2 | Black Hole Pendant | Spell | Rainbow |
| 1 | Blood Transfusion | Spell | Rainbow |
| 2 | Furious Rooster | Creature | NiceLands |
| 2 | Music Mallard | Creature | NiceLands |
| 2 | Cottonpult | Creature | NiceLands |
| 2 | Dr. Stuffenstein | Creature | NiceLands |
| 2 | Furious Hen | Creature | NiceLands |
| 2 | Papercut Tiger | Creature | NiceLands |
| 1 | Bog Ban-She Angel | Creature | Useless Swamp |
| 2 | Pentaid | Spell | NiceLands |
| 1 | Auto-Plucker | Building | NiceLands |
| 1 | The Big Hen House | Building | NiceLands |
| 2 | Ban-She Princess | Creature | Useless Swamp |
| 2 | Fly Swatter | Creature | Useless Swamp |
| 2 | Bog Bum | Creature | Useless Swamp |
| 2 | Unicyclops | Creature | Useless Swamp |
| 2 | Man-Witch | Creature | Useless Swamp |
| 1 | Ban-She Queen | Creature | Useless Swamp |
| 1 | Bog Frog Bomb | Creature | Useless Swamp |
| 2 | Bums Away! | Spell | Useless Swamp |
| 2 | Blood Bath | Spell | Useless Swamp |
| 1 | Funeral Home | Building | Useless Swamp |
| 1 | Cardboard Mansion | Building | Useless Swamp |

**Auto-Plucker** is the key card in the ATK boost strategy. It boosts your Furious fowl Creatures, pinpoints the correct amount of Damage on the Creatures that get a big boost on a certain amount of Damage, and keeps your Creatures alive when their DEF gets low. Because it's a Building, it's less likely than a Creature to be destroyed by your opponent, which means you can reliably Floop it every turn.

**Unicyclops** will improve your opponent's hand over time, so the goal with this Creature is to punish your opponent for discarding cards. There are plenty of ways to do that in Marceline's Nice/Swamp deck, but Unicyclops is a card that ensures you'll get a discard from your opponent every turn.

**The Big Hen House** speeds up your ATK bonuses and keeps you healthy and full of Hit Points.

# Marceline's NiceLands/Useless Swamp Deck Payoffs

These three Furious fowl will seriously mess up your opponent. You can enable their ATK boost with your Damage-dealing abilities, but they will work just fine on their own. It's not uncommon to get in a hit with 6 or 7 points of Damage from **Furious Rooster** and **Furious Hen**.

**Cardboard Mansion** is difficult to play, and requires a very full discard pile before it can be played, but once it's out there, its value is real. Being able to draw an extra card or play an extra Creature every turn feels like cheating, and in this case, cheaters usually do win.

**Man-Witch** is the real juicy payoff for making your opponent discard cards.

# Marceline's NiceLands/Useless Swamp Deck Combos

**Cottonpult** is an insane card, definitely one of the best Creatures in the game. You Floop to deal 1 Damage to any Creature (that means you can move your own ATK-boost Creatures to their sweet spot, or weaken your enemy). The crazy thing is, if you have 5 or more Damage on it, Cottonpult heals 1 Damage and readies, meaning you can Floop again, heal another Damage, ready again, until you have less than 5 Damage on Cottonpult. **Auto-Plucker** ensures you can Floop twice every turn, heal up, and mow down your opponent's Creatures without Cottonpult ever being in danger of going to the discard pile. This combo also works with **The Big Hen House**. Speaking of which . . .

**Bog Ban-She Angel** is the kind of Creature that takes over a game. Timed correctly, Bog Ban-She Angel's ability allows you to deal massive amounts of Damage to an opponent's Creature. Some opponents will avoid her entirely, because they know she is so powerful after she gets hit. **The Big Hen House** guarantees that she will always have Damage on her, allowing you to smack your opponent's Creatures whether they like it or not.

Like several other decks, Marceline's deck is tugging you in two directions. First, it wants to make your opponent discard cards. Second, it wants to Damage its own Creatures to enable super-powered Attacks. Your goal in improving the deck should be to focus on one of these two strategies.

For ATK-boost Creatures, look to Princess Bubblegum's deck. **Ms. Fluff** is one among many potential additions. A good enabler from that deck is **Apple Pieclops**, which will help you hit, and stay on, each Creature's sweet spot. **Nice Windmill**, from the booster pack, does this as well, for a small Action cost.

Lumpy Space Princess's deck and BMO's deck have strong additions to this deck's discard strategy, including **Skeletal Hand** for filling up your discard pile, **Abraca Amadeus** for making your opponent discard, and **Chest Burster** for thumping your opponent once their hand is empty.

If you want raw power, look to the cards found in For the Glory! Booster Pack, including **Raise the Dead, Smoldering Elder**, and **Sack of Pain**.

# Lemongrab's Cornfield/SandyLands Deck

So, you want to hear about Lemongrab's deck that has both Cornfield and SandyLands, do you? Eh? Well then, listen closely and I'll tell you about it. Listen! Or I'll send you to the dungeon. DUNGEEEEEON! Forty years dungeon! One year for every card in my deck. You can find this deck in the Lemongrab vs. Gunter Collector's Pack. It's . . . mmmm, delicious! With this deck, corn gets its revenge! The Pig and other nasties have been Flooping my beloved Cornfield for too long. Now corn takes the Flooping to its enemies. Yes! My Creatures get more powerful when the opponent has facedown Landscapes. Hehehehehe! It's a ravenous strategy in the same way that I am also ravenous, haha!

I find your silence to be acceptable. I bequeath you this lovely Parrotrooper. What's that?! Is the Parrotrooper *terrible* and ruining your day? Well, too bad! That's what I had planned all along.

# Decklist

| Number in Deck | Name | Type | Landscape |
|---|---|---|---|
| 1 | Ol' Corn Eye | Creature | Cornfield |
| 2 | Fancy Zebracorn | Creature | Cornfield |
| 2 | Rebounding Zebracorn | Creature | Cornfield |
| 1 | Bouncing Zebracorn | Creature | Cornfield |
| 2 | Mantle Masher | Creature | Cornfield |
| 2 | Rock 'n Roller | Creature | Cornfield |
| 2 | Quake Maker | Creature | Cornfield |
| 1 | Earth Mover | Creature | Cornfield |
| 2 | Rock Out! | Spell | Rainbow |
| 1 | Amaizing Avalanche | Spell | Cornfield |
| 1 | Sinkhole | Building | Cornfield |
| 1 | Silo of Freedom | Building | Cornfield |
| 1 | Carmel Camel | Creature | SandyLands |
| 2 | Ska-pion | Creature | SandyLands |
| 1 | Sandmagus | Creature | SandyLands |
| 1 | Grand Mummy | Creature | SandyLands |
| 1 | Sandasaurus Rex | Creature | SandyLands |
| 2 | Static Parrotrooper | Creature | Rainbow |
| 2 | Jinxed Parrotrooper | Creature | Rainbow |
| 1 | Husky Parrotrooper | Creature | Rainbow |
| 1 | Dragoon Parrotrooper | Creature | Rainbow |
| 2 | Drop Zone | Spell | Rainbow |
| 1 | Quick Pick Me Up | Spell | SandyLands |
| 1 | Parrotmilitary Outpost | Building | Rainbow |
| 1 | Lunchpad | Building | SandyLands |
| 2 | TNTimmy | Creature | Rainbow |
| 1 | Ham Fist | Spell | Rainbow |
| 2 | Freefall | Spell | SandyLands |

Boulder boys, smash! **Mantle Masher** and **Rock 'n Roller** are two Creatures that serve the same purpose. They flip over your opponent's Landscapes. Against decks with multiple Landscape types, this can be devastating, and there are Creatures in Lemongrab's deck that *loooooove* facedown Landscapes, making Mantle Masher and Rock 'n Roller stone-cold stompers.

The **Parrotroopers** are like giving a cold to your opponent. You've got it, and then you hand it over. Remember, when it says "move it to any empty Landscape," it's talking about your opponent's Landscapes. They lose the ability to play Creatures in that Lane. Lemongrab's deck gives you all sorts of bonuses for using the Parrotroopers. More on that in the Payoff section.

**Sinkhole** is a consistent way to lock down on one of your opponent's Landscapes, as well as give a boost to your Creatures who care about facedown Landscapes.

The **Zebracorns** are aggressive Creatures that get even stronger when you have multiple Landscape types. Lemongrab's deck has two types, which is good, but if you are crazy enough to play a deck with three or four different types, these Creatures will look like they eat all their vegetables.

**Quake Maker** and **Earth Mover** are giving the deck's other rock giants a run for their pebbles. These Creatures get an ATK boost for each facedown Landscape in play (yours and your opponent's). That means that Quake Maker could potentially go all the way up to 15 ATK, 7 DEF (leaving one Cornfield faceup so you can play the card cost). Now those stats are pretty pieclops in the sky, but a boulder boy can dream, can't he?

**Sandasaurus Rex** takes advantage of all your empty Lanes, hitting your opponent for massive Damage.

**Amaizing Avalanche** gives all your Creatures a boost depending on how many facedown Landscapes are in play. Run for the hills! Oh wait, somebody flipped the hills facedown.

**Ska-pion** is a nice aggressive Creature made even better if your opponent controls a Creature you own. Good thing the Parrotroopers fit the bill. (Or is that *beak*?) **Dragoon Parrotrooper** is the best here. Even though he costs 2 Actions to play, he allows you to play Ska-pion for 0 Actions, getting a little extra oomph from your combo. Dragoon Parrotrooper's side effect might also help keep Ska-pion around longer by weakening your opponent's ATK.

**Ham Fist** is not a very good card, but it has its uses. You can use it to keep your Parrotroopers on enemy turf for a longer amount of time. It also allows you to change whose turn a Creature will be destroyed on, and that often matters.

Lemongrab's Cornfield/SandyLands deck has a pretty focused strategy, but there are a few additions that can make the deck even stronger. Jake's Cornfield deck has **Legion of Earlings**, which opens space on your opponent's side to play a **Static Parrotrooper**. Lady Rainicorn's SandyLands deck has **Beach Mummy**—a powerful utility Creature that can return your own Creatures to hand—and **Tome of Ankhs**, which rewards you with extra cards by having empty Lanes. Then there's **Lady Beetle** from the For the Glory! Booster Pack. She helps return your Creatures to your hand when their DEF gets low.

# Gunter's Blue Plains/ IcyLands Deck

*Wenk! Wennnnk! \*flaps arms\* WENK!*

BAD GUNTER! Use your words. Sorry about that. Gunter here was trying to tell you about his Blue Plains/IcyLands deck from the Lemongrab vs. Gunter Collector's Pack. It's a very clever deck that Freezes Landscapes like nobody's biz, and then pummels opponents with giant Blue Plains Creatures. Ah, it brings an icy tear to my eye to see Snowmen and their Woadic allies putting the hurt on decks everywhere. Heh. You know, you didn't ask but I want to tell you, anyway: The thing I like most about Gunter's deck is that his IcyLands cards are more controlling than the IcyLands cards in *my* aggressive IcyLands deck, and the Blue Plains cards are more aggressive than Finn's very controlling Blue Plains deck. Just goes to snow (er, show), you should never judge a Landscape by its cover.

*Wenk!*

# Decklist

| Number in Deck | Name | Type | Landscape |
|---|---|---|---|
| 2 | Snow Baller | Creature | IcyLands |
| 1 | Frosted Snowwoman | Creature | IcyLands |
| 1 | The Cooler | Creature | IcyLands |
| 1 | Glacier Racer | Creature | IcyLands |
| 2 | Frosted Deanimator | Creature | IcyLands |
| 2 | Icy Infiltrator | Spell | Rainbow |
| 2 | Snowblower | Spell | IcyLands |
| 2 | Icy Commando | Creature | IcyLands |
| 2 | Icy Intruder | Creature | IcyLands |
| 2 | Snowvalanche | Spell | Rainbow |
| 1 | Floating Ice Palace | Building | IcyLands |
| 1 | Snow Training Camp | Building | Rainbow |
| 2 | Industrial Assassin | Creature | Blue Plains |
| 2 | Tired Wombat | Creature | Blue Plains |
| 2 | Fatigued Librarian | Creature | Blue Plains |
| 2 | Woadic Ring Leader | Creature | Blue Plains |
| 2 | Weakened Warrior | Creature | Blue Plains |
| 2 | Drained Cleric | Creature | Blue Plains |
| 1 | Wake Up Call | Spell | Blue Plains |
| 2 | Spazzy Cola | Spell | Rainbow |
| 2 | Tapped Out | Spell | Blue Plains |
| 1 | Cute Overload | Spell | Rainbow |
| 1 | Weary Trading Post | Building | Rainbow |
| 1 | Fancy Spa | Building | Blue Plains |
| 1 | Magenapping | Spell | Blue Plains |

Gunter's deck gets its power from Frozen Tokens, which, thanks to the other Creatures in your deck, won't hurt you as much as they hurt your opponent. **Frosted Snowwoman** is one cool lady. She exemplifies this mirrored Frozen Token effect (but the mirrored effect won't treat you and your opponent equally).

Sometimes you'll run into a situation where one of your Creatures would get a bonus from being on a Landscape with a Frozen Token, but you need to get rid of the Frozen Token to play the Creature. **Snowblower** solves that problem. Play your Creature first, then play Snowblower to lock out your opponent and get the bonus.

**Icy Intruder** is a repeatable source of Frozen Tokens, making him one of the most important and consistent cards in Gunter's deck.

**Weary Trading Post** can wake up your powerful Blue Plains Creatures that enter play exhausted.

**Snow Baller** takes advantage of all the Frozen tokens your cards will put on your Landscapes, turning them into Damage you can throw at your opponent's Creatures. That big a hit will change the math in any Fight, so use the ability early and often.

Plenty of cards in your deck Freeze both Landscapes in a single Lane, and **Glacier Racer** makes it worth your while. The dream is to play Glacier Racer onto an empty Lane, and then follow it up immediately with Snowblower. That turn you'll get in for 6 Damage, and your opponent will need to spend two cards just to get in the way of your Creature.

You'll win hearty high fives from your friends if you can make **Icy Commando** a 9 ATK, 7 DEF Creature.

**Magenapping** rewards you for playing a controlling deck.

**Weakened Warrior** packs a huge punch, and is at its best when you get to Fight with it. Using **Wake Up Call** with a few of these exhausted Creatures in play is one of the simpler combos in the deck, but it's still effective.

One of the frustrating things about playing with lots of Frozen Tokens is that you can't play Creatures onto Frozen Landscapes unless you discard cards to remove the tokens. But sometimes you don't want to get rid of the tokens, even though you want to play a Creature in that Lane. **Woadic Ring Leader** and Creatures like him skate around this problem by allowing you to move them to empty Lanes that have Frozen Tokens on them, as long as you have an unfrozen Landscape to play them on in the first place.

# Gunter's Blue Plains/ IcyLands Deck Improvements

**Dragon Claw**
1

Blue Plains Creature

FLOOP >>> Move a Creature you control to an empty Lane.

1 / 8

**Gnome Snot**
1

Blue Plains Spell

Draw 3 cards.

**Sprucy Lucy**
2

IcyLands Creature

Sprucy Lucy has +1 ATK for each Landscape with a Frozen token on it players control.

2 / 9

**Reign Deer**
2

IcyLands Creature

FLOOP >>> Draw a card for each Landscape with a Frozen token on it players control.

4 / 4

**Paladim**
2

Blue Plains Creature

Each Creature that changed Lanes this turn has +3 ATK this turn. *(Opposing Creatures do not benefit from this.)*

3 / 7

**Dragon Claw** will help move your Creatures between Lanes more easily, while **Gnome Snot** will keep the cards flowing, as both you and your opponent will be discarding a lot of them to remove Frozen Tokens. Both cards can be found in Finn's Blue Plains deck. For powerful Creatures, look to **Sprucy Lucy** and **Reign Deer**, both found in Ice King's IcyLands deck. The For the Glory! Booster Pack also has a few good options, such as **Paladim**, who will give an extra boost to your creatures who have moved Lanes.

# Fionna's Blue Plains Deck

Hey, weirdos! I'm here to teach you about my Blue Plains deck and junk! The key to this deck is making all your Creatures into Rainbow Creatures, then powering up those Rainbow Creatures, and then punching your opponent in the face for a million points! For example, throw down a **Pony**, drop a **Crazy Cat Lady**, and then send that Pony galloping to victory! Your Pony will have 2 ATK instead of 1 ATK. The deck has another sweet bonus, too. A bunch of cards in the deck, like **Singing Sword**, give you a bonus for every card you draw in a turn. You can use cards like **Glorious Gramophone** to get a huge advantage!

# Decklist

| Number in Deck | Name | Type | Landscape |
| --- | --- | --- | --- |
| 2 | Pony | Creature | Rainbow |
| 2 | The Dog | Creature | Rainbow |
| 2 | Lonely Panda | Creature | Blue Plains |
| 2 | Infant Scholar | Creature | Blue Plains |
| 2 | Tiny Elephant | Creature | Blue Plains |
| 1 | Woadic Matriarch | Creature | Blue Plains |
| 2 | Psionic Swashbuckler | Creature | Blue Plains |
| 1 | Business Dog | Creature | Blue Plains |
| 1 | Fiddling Ferret | Creature | Blue Plains |
| 2 | Woadic Weirdo | Creature | Blue Plains |
| 1 | Vampire Lord | Creature | Rainbow |
| 2 | Emboldened Retriever | Creature | Blue Plains |
| 2 | Crazy Cat Lady | Creature | Blue Plains |
| 2 | Impossible Possum | Creature | Blue Plains |
| 2 | Woadic Enchantress | Creature | Blue Plains |
| 2 | Friendship Bracelet | Spell | Rainbow |
| 2 | Singing Sword | Spell | Rainbow |
| 2 | Sword Bouquet | Spell | Rainbow |
| 2 | Glorious Gramophone | Spell | Blue Plains |
| 1 | River of Swords | Spell | Rainbow |
| 1 | Puppy Parade | Spell | Blue Plains |
| 1 | Charming City | Building | Blue Plains |
| 1 | Learning Center | Building | Blue Plains |
| 2 | Oil Refinery | Building | Blue Plains |

It isn't typical for 1-Action Rainbow Creatures to have good stats like 2 ATK, 6 DEF, but **Tiny Elephant** makes it work by keeping one foot in the Blue Plains world and another in Rainbow. Cards like this will increase the total number of Rainbow Creatures in your deck. This way you can get the most value out of your payoff cards.

**Tiny Elephant**

1

**Blue Plains Creature**

While in play, Tiny Elephant is also a Rainbow Creature. (In addition to Blue Plains.)

2 / 6

What's better than turning one of your Creatures into a Rainbow Creature? Turning ALL your Creatures into Rainbow Creatures. **Puppy Parade** does just that, and the healing ability is nothing to sneeze at, either.

**Puppy Parade**

2

**Blue Plains Spell**

Heal 2 Damage from each Creature you control. Creatures you control lose their Landscape type and become Rainbow Creatures this turn.

**Glorious Gramophone**

1

**Blue Plains Spell**

Draw 4 cards, then discard 2 cards.

Gaining card advantage is always a good way to have an edge over your opponent, but **Glorious Gramophone** is even better than it seems. This deck rewards you for drawing lots of cards, even if you don't get to keep them all in your hand.

If you're wondering why you want so many Rainbow Creatures, **Woadic Matriarch** will want to have a word. She gets +1 ATK for each Rainbow Creature you control, which means that, at most, she can be a 4 ATK, 7 DEF and only costs 1 Action to play. (Hot tip: If you can somehow make Woadic Matriarch herself a Rainbow Creature, she can have 5 ATK!)

**Infant Scholar** is another aggressive Creature that gets more powerful if you play a Rainbow card. Two things to remember: You can play a Rainbow Creature or Spell to get this effect, but only once per turn. If you play two Rainbow cards, you will still only get +3 ATK.

**Singing Sword** and **Sword Bouquet** will help you deal some serious damage whenever you draw cards, which happens pretty often in this deck.

# Fionna's Blue Plains Deck
## Combos

The Floop abilities on **Fiddling Ferret** and **Woadic Weirdo** form a neato combo. First, Floop Woadic Weirdo, and reveal the worst card in your hand. That card becomes Rainbow. Next, Floop Fiddling Ferret, draw a card, and discard the card you revealed with Woadic Weirdo. You'll always draw a fresh card and always gain 1 Action.

**Friendship Bracelet** is a cute Spell, but it doesn't do much for you. If you have 3 Damage on a Creature before you play the Spell, you're still going to have 3 Damage on a Creature afterward. **Vampire Lord** says "Nuh uh" to this problem. Whenever he attacks, he heals himself. If you set this up right, you can move Damage from one Creature onto Vampire Lord, and then heal that Damage up. Sweet!

94

The best decks work well because the cards have synergy with one another. While the stuff this deck does is cool, you should really choose which game plan you want to pursue—the card draw plan or the Rainbow Creature plan. Then add cards that help that plan, and take out cards that don't. Here are a few directions you can go.

If you choose to go the card draw route, you will want cards like **Gnome Snot** in your deck. Holy cow, it draws you a bunch of cards!

If you choose to fill your deck with more Rainbow Creature cards, borrow some copies of **The Pig** from Finn's Blue Plains deck. It's especially good against Cake's Cornfield deck.

**Well-Dressed Wolf** has powerful stats, and it's even better against a Cornfield deck. Including it with your Rainbow Creature deck is a no-brainer!

# Cake's Cornfield Deck

Hey there, studly girlfriends and boyfriends! I'm here to tell you all about my *gor-gee-us* Cornfield deck. Maybe you've played a different Cornfield deck already, but I guarantee this one ain't like no other Cornfield deck you've played. My deck is all about using Buildings and powerful Floop effects to control your opponent's Landscapes. You can play Creatures like **Burly Lumberjack** and **Tornado Wall of Fire,** which have super-high DEF and can resist many attacks. These Creatures will buy you time to set up your **Cabin of Many Woods** and **Blood Castle**. Once you have Buildings on all your Landscapes, your opponent's Creatures are in for a world of hurt. The goal is to outlast your opponent and then push through for a big win!

# Decklist

| Number in Deck | Name | Type | Landscape |
|---|---|---|---|
| 2 | Helping Hand | Creature | Rainbow |
| 2 | Hunkclops | Creature | Rainbow |
| 2 | Lumbercaddy | Creature | Cornfield |
| 2 | Husker Champion | Creature | Cornfield |
| 2 | Druid of the Cob | Creature | Cornfield |
| 2 | Popcorn Butteredfly | Creature | Cornfield |
| 2 | Burly Lumberjack | Creature | Cornfield |
| 2 | Corns Templar | Creature | Cornfield |
| 1 | Sharp Guy | Creature | Cornfield |
| 1 | Kernel Queen | Creature | Cornfield |
| 2 | Husker Valkyrie | Creature | Cornfield |
| 2 | Tough Lumberjill | Creature | Cornfield |
| 1 | Archer Danica | Creature | Cornfield |
| 2 | Pied Piper | Creature | Cornfield |
| 2 | Tornado Wall of Fire | Creature | Cornfield |
| 1 | Void Thimble | Spell | Rainbow |
| 2 | Furious Furor | Spell | Cornfield |
| 2 | Log Rhythm | Spell | Cornfield |
| 1 | Harvest Moon | Spell | Cornfield |
| 1 | Deforestation | Spell | Cornfield |
| 2 | Celestial Fortress | Building | Rainbow |
| 2 | Blood Castle | Building | Rainbow |
| 1 | Farmhouse | Building | Cornfield |
| 1 | Cabin of Many Woods | Building | Cornfield |

Many of the Creatures in my Cornfield deck get bonuses if you control Buildings and/or Flooped Creatures. **Helping Hand** lends a helping hand to both, as it can Floop itself and retrieve your Buildings from your discard pile.

In addition to providing a Floop Creature for many of the deck's payoff cards, **Sharp Guy** can slice two points of DEF off your opponent's Creature each turn, helping your game plan of controlling the Landscapes.

The best "Additional Costs" are secretly additional benefits. That's the case with this **Deforestation** Spell, where getting to Floop one of your Creatures goes along with your game plan. Being able to dig up your best Building out of your deck is pretty sweet, too.

**Tough Lumberjill** is a great way to finish off an opponent once you get a Building onto all four of your Landscapes. Smack your opponent for 4 Damage immediately, and then clock them for 3 per turn.

In a deck where you're trying to draw and play as many Buildings as you can, **Popcorn Butteredfly** gives you HUGE card advantage. HUGE, I tell you. That steady stream of cards will ensure that you have a Creature and a Building on each of your Landscapes for the duration of the game.

**Husker Valkyrie** will almost always have 4 ATK and 8 DEF in your deck with so many Buildings. You don't need to be reminded how powerful 4 ATK can be. Guaranteed, once you've attacked your opponent with this card, you'll love the smell of Cornfield in the morning.

Heavy Damage, when each of your opponent's Creatures is dealt Damage from a single source at once, is one of the most powerful effects in all of Card Wars. But **Archer Danica**'s heavy Damage Floop ability comes at a real cost: the destruction of an essential Building. **Harvest Moon** allows you to buy back your Building from the discard pile, dodging Danica's downside and making this a killer combo.

**Tornado Wall of Fire** works great with the deck's strategy to slow the game down and build up a defensive advantage, but with 10 DEF, you really want Tornado Wall of Fire to get out there and punch face. (Remember, Flooped Creatures don't attack.) **Pied Piper** can coax Tornado Wall into attacking with its ability; Just don't forget to Floop Tornado Wall first!

# Cake's Cornfield Deck
## Improvements

Knock your opponent on their ears (of corn) with the powerful **Patchy the Pumpkin** from Jake's Cornfield deck. This deck also has a bunch of Cornfield Landscapes and cares about Floop abilities to boot!

**Wall of Ears** is a good defensive Creature for early in the game, and it loves Cornfield Landscapes. You can find it in Jake's Cornfield deck.

**Archer Dan** gives you another Cornfield Creature with a Floop ability, and he will ensure that you maintain Building dominance over your opponent. You can find Archer Dan in Jake's Cornfield deck.

**Patchy the Pumpkin** — 1

Cornfield Creature

FLOOP >>> Deal 1 Damage to target Creature. Do this once for each Cornfield Landscape you control. (May only target each Creature once.)

0 / 5

**Wall of Ears** — 1

Cornfield Creature

+1 DEF for each Cornfield Landscape in play (counting all players).

2 / 4

**Archer Dan** — 2

Cornfield Creature

FLOOP >>> Destroy target Building in Archer Dan's Lane.

2 / 6

# Tips for Deckbuilding

Hey, dudes, didja miss me? Your old pal Jake hasn't talked to ya in a while. So here goes, Jake's Awesome Rules for Building Awesome Decks. You can build sweet creations as cool as the ones you find in this book. *And between you and me, I think you can make some even cooler!* So listen up, I'm gonna give you some top secret deckcrafting strategy.

The minimum number of cards in your deck is 40. You can have as many cards more than that as you want, but you should **never put more than 40 cards in a deck**. Think about it like this: When you draw the top card of your deck, you have a 1-in-40 chance of drawing your deck's best card. If you have 41 cards in your deck, you are *less* likely to draw your best card than if you have 40. If you have *50* cards in your deck—oh man, don't even get me started!

Similarly, the maximum number of copies of a card you can have in a deck is 3. You should almost *always* put 3 copies of your best cards in your deck. Same reason as above. More copies, and you are more likely to draw the card you need.

Have a plan. What does your deck want to do? Attack early and often? Slow the game down, play blockers, and then overwhelm your opponent with card advantage? Maybe it wants to do something weird like discard its whole hand to power up its Creatures. Whatever you decide, make sure to focus your card choices on the things that lead you directly to that goal.

Extra types of Landscapes have a cost. That cost is consistency, and if your opponent has Landscape-flipping effects in their deck, you could be in serious danger of not being able to play your cards. If you're making a deck with 3+ Landscape types, look at the Landscape with the fewest cards of its type. Could these cards be replaced by similar effects in your other Landscape types?

Check the balance of Creatures to not-Creatures in your deck. If you have too many fancy Spells and Buildings, you run the risk of not having enough of a defense to stop your opponent. When starting out, try to keep the ratio of 3 Creatures for every 1 Spell or Building. Most decks should have 28–30 Creatures and 10–12 Spells.

Make sure you have a good mix of 1-Action and 2-Action Creatures, and a few 0-Action Creatures as well. It's tempting to put a bunch of the 2-Action Creatures in your deck because the 2-Action Creatures always look so SWEET, but it takes time to play the expensive guys, and an aggressive opponent will run you over big time.

There are a lot of cards that are powerful *but only in very specific circumstances*. Put these in your sideboard (more about that later), not your main deck. As much as Finn loves The Pig, he knows to only bring it in against an opponent with Cornfield Landscapes. The For the Glory! Booster Pack has a bunch of Rainbow Creatures that hate on specific Landscape types, and Spells of many varieties that give a bonus against certain Landscape types, but these cards don't belong in your main deck. They won't be effective against a majority of opponents who aren't running those Landscape types.

And of course these little Gnome guys are cute and all, but they're only worth it in very specific situations.

Okay, amigos, deep breath. It's time to start building your very own decks. If you want to smash all your decks together and lay the cards out on the floor or table, that's cool. If you want to put the old decks back together, you've got the complete decklists for each here in this book. So go ahead! I've provided you with five awesome custom-built decks that I've found to be pretty tried and true. After that there are some blank pages for you to write in your own custom decks. When you turn the page, you'll see that I've started you off with your very first deck. Good luck!

# CUSTOM DECKS

## Corn/Swamp Beatdown!

**Immortal Maize Walker**

**2**

Useless Swamp Creature

While Immortal Maize Walker is on a Cornfield Landscape, it deals triple Damage.

**2** / **8**

This custom deck has it all: strong starting Creatures, game-breaking powerful Creatures, Corn/Swamp synergies, card draw, Creature removal, and ways to retrieve your Creatures from the discard pile. Balancing so many elements can be tricky, but this build ensures that you will be able to withstand early pressure and overwhelm your opponent later on.

**Landscapes:** Useless Swamp/Cornfield/Useless Swamp/Cornfield

Landscape

**Useless Swamp**

Landscape

**Cornfield**

Landscape

**Useless Swamp**

Landscape

**Cornfield**

**Hero Card:**
Magic Man

**Magic Man**

When you play a card with cost exactly 2, deal 2 Damage to a Creature an opponent controls.

# Decklist

| Number in Deck | Name | Type | Landscape |
|---|---|---|---|
| 3 | Red Eyeling | Creature | Useless Swamp |
| 3 | Lt. Mushroom | Creature | Useless Swamp |
| 3 | Immortal Maize Walker | Creature | Useless Swamp |
| 2 | Green Merman | Creature | Useless Swamp |
| 2 | Tree of Undeath | Creature | Useless Swamp |
| 2 | Bog Ban-She Angel | Creature | Useless Swamp |
| 2 | Dr. Death | Creature | Useless Swamp |
| 3 | Corn Dog | Creature | Cornfield |
| 3 | Pirate Bear | Creature | Cornfield |
| 3 | Corn Ronin | Creature | Cornfield |
| 2 | Field Reaper | Creature | Cornfield |
| 1 | Archer Dan | Creature | Cornfield |
| 3 | Raise the Dead | Spell | Useless Swamp |
| 2 | Snake Eye Ring | Spell | Rainbow |
| 2 | Unempty Coffin | Spell | Rainbow |
| 2 | Bone Wand | Spell | Rainbow |
| 2 | Blood Fortress | Building | Rainbow |

# Nice/Sandy Skewer

What makes the NiceLands deck strong is the ability to give its Creatures an ATK boost when they have a certain amount of Damage on them, or no Damage at all. But there are two problems. First, the no-Damage Creatures only get in one powerful hit before they take Damage. Second, when the Creatures finally whittle down their DEF to the right number for an ATK boost, an opponent's Creature gets in the way. Adding SandyLands cards solves both problems. You get effects that return your opponent's Creatures to hand, clearing the path so you can skewer your opponent with a big, boosted Attack, and you get effects that return your own Creatures to hand, so you can replay them *Damage-free*. Two SandyLands Creatures that like NiceLands—**Sand Jackal** and **Diamond Dan** from the For the Glory! Booster Pack—tie the whole deck together.

**Landscapes:** NiceLands/SandyLands/NiceLands/SandyLands

## Hero Card:
Princess Bubblegum

# Decklist

| Number in Deck | Name | Type | Landscape |
|---|---|---|---|
| 3 | Cottonpult | Creature | NiceLands |
| 3 | Furious Rooster | Creature | NiceLands |
| 2 | Ms. Fluff | Creature | NiceLands |
| 2 | Wall of Chocolate | Creature | NiceLands |
| 2 | Niceasaurus Rex | Creature | NiceLands |
| 2 | Apple Pieclops | Creature | NiceLands |
| 2 | Sack of Pain | Creature | NiceLands |
| 3 | Beach Mummy | Creature | SandyLands |
| 3 | Fummy | Creature | SandyLands |
| 3 | Sand Jackal | Creature | SandyLands |
| 3 | Diamond Dan | Creature | SandyLands |
| 2 | Sandsnake | Creature | SandyLands |
| 2 | Sandhorn Devil | Creature | SandyLands |
| 1 | Ms. Mummy | Creature | Rainbow |
| 2 | Piestorm | Spell | NiceLands |
| 1 | Portal of Unsummoning | Spell | SandyLands |
| 2 | Windmill of Health | Building | NiceLands |
| 2 | Sand Sphinx | Building | SandyLands |

# Icy/Swamp Lockdown

This snowy swamp is one of the most controlling decks out there. That means it is slow, but once it gets ahead, your opponent won't be able to do anything at all. The plan here is to combine the Frozen Tokens of the IcyLands with the discard effects of the Useless Swamp to eat up your opponent's entire hand. Soon, they won't have any cards to discard to get rid of your Frozen Tokens, which means they can't play the Creatures in their hand. Once your opponent is locked out like this, your Creatures can Attack unobstructed.

**Landscapes:** IcyLands/Useless Swamp/IcyLands/Useless Swamp

**Hero Card:**
Ricardio

# Decklist

| Number in Deck | Name | Type | Landscape |
|---|---|---|---|
| 3 | Black Paladin | Creature | Useless Swamp |
| 3 | Lt. Mushroom | Creature | Useless Swamp |
| 3 | Bog Bum | Creature | Useless Swamp |
| 3 | Chest Buster | Creature | Useless Swamp |
| 2 | Blue Merlock | Creature | Useless Swamp |
| 2 | Smoldering Elder | Creature | Useless Swamp |
| 2 | Unicyclops | Creature | Useless Swamp |
| 2 | Man-Witch | Creature | Useless Swamp |
| 2 | Mace Stump | Creature | Useless Swamp |
| 1 | Skeletal Hand | Creature | Useless Swamp |
| 1 | Green Merman | Creature | Useless Swamp |
| 2 | Frost Dragon | Creature | IcyLands |
| 2 | Frozen Fish | Creature | IcyLands |
| 3 | Wandering Bald Man | Creature | Rainbow |
| 1 | Raise the Dead | Spell | Useless Swamp |
| 3 | Freeze Ray | Spell | IcyLands |
| 2 | Frosty Frolic | Spell | IcyLands |
| 2 | Freezing Point | Spell | IcyLands |
| 1 | Snow Way | Spell | IcyLands |

# Blue/Corn Deck Draw

What if there was a way to defeat your opponent without ever Fighting? Now it is possible, with this sleek Blue Plains/Cornfield deck that is all about drawing cards, and the Billy Hero Card. Billy's card says that when your opponent's deck is empty, you win the game. You help them speed up the process by forcing them to draw way more cards than they could ever use, and then smashing them for huge amounts of Damage with cards like Travelin' Farmer and Field of Nightmares. Use your Heavenly Gazer to replay Field of Nightmares and Strength Crystal (targeting your opponent, of course), and soon your opponent will be wincing every time they take a card from their ever-thinner deck.

**Landscapes:** Cornfield/Blue Plains/Cornfield/Blue Plains

**Hero Card:**
Billy

# Decklist

| Number in Deck | Name | Type | Landscape |
|---|---|---|---|
| 3 | Heavenly Gazer | Creature | Blue Plains |
| 3 | Djini Ghost | Creature | Blue Plains |
| 2 | Cool Dog | Creature | Blue Plains |
| 3 | Travelin' Farmer | Creature | Cornfield |
| 3 | Legion of Earlings | Creature | Cornfield |
| 3 | Field Stalker | Creature | Cornfield |
| 3 | Corn Dog | Creature | Cornfield |
| 2 | Field Reaper | Creature | Cornfield |
| 3 | Quadurai | Creature | Rainbow |
| 3 | Strength Crystal | Spell | Blue Plains |
| 3 | Field of Nightmares | Spell | Cornfield |
| 2 | Witch Slap | Spell | Rainbow |
| 3 | Yellow Lighthouse | Building | Cornfield |
| 2 | Silo of Justice | Building | Cornfield |
| 2 | Celestial Castle | Building | Rainbow |

# Rainbow Slimey Attack

Slimeys are mean. Super mean. These little cubes of crud don't play favorites when it comes to Landscapes; in fact, they're at their best when you have three or more different types of Landscapes in play. The major drawback is that your deck can't have any non-Rainbow cards that cost more than 1 Action to play, but that doesn't matter, because your goal here is to unload as many Creatures as quickly as possible. Each Slimey comes with a powerful bonus, and the rest of the cards in the deck are either similarly aggressive or focused on getting more of these Creatures into your hand, either through card draw or returning a Slimey to your hand to replay. Watch your friends weep *slimey* tears of sorrow as you charge with Rainbow Slimey Attack.

**Landscapes:** Cornfield/Blue Plains/Useless Swamp/SandyLands

**Hero Card:**
Prismo

# Decklist

| Number in Deck | Name | Type | Landscape |
|---|---|---|---|
| 3 | Lime Slimey | Creature | SandyLands |
| 3 | Sand Knights | Creature | SandyLands |
| 3 | Beach Mummy | Creature | SandyLands |
| 2 | Lady Beetle | Creature | SandyLands |
| 3 | Blue Slimey | Creature | Blue Plains |
| 3 | Orange Slimey | Creature | Useless Swamp |
| 3 | Fisher Fish | Creature | Useless Swamp |
| 3 | Yellow Slimey | Creature | Cornfield |
| 3 | Gold Ninja | Creature | Cornfield |
| 3 | Corn Bat | Creature | Cornfield |
| 2 | Psychic Tempest | Spell | SandyLands |
| 3 | Gnome Snot | Spell | Blue Plains |
| 1 | Grape Butt | Spell | Cornfield |
| 2 | Ring of Damage | Spell | Rainbow |
| 2 | Blood Fortress | Building | Rainbow |

# Decklist

Ready to start customizing? Here are a few corny cards to get you started.

## JAKE AND _____'S CORN CRUSHER!

| Number in Deck | Name | Type | Landscape |
|---|---|---|---|
| 3 | Husker Knight | Creature | Cornfield |
| 3 | Cornataur | Creature | Cornfield |
|  |  |  |  |
|  |  |  |  |
|  |  |  |  |
|  |  |  |  |
|  |  |  |  |
|  |  |  |  |
|  |  |  |  |
|  |  |  |  |
|  |  |  |  |
|  |  |  |  |
|  |  |  |  |
|  |  |  |  |
|  |  |  |  |
|  |  |  |  |
|  |  |  |  |

# Decklist

Deck name: _____

| Number in Deck | Name | Type | Landscape |
|---|---|---|---|
| | | | |
| | | | |
| | | | |
| | | | |
| | | | |
| | | | |
| | | | |
| | | | |
| | | | |
| | | | |
| | | | |
| | | | |
| | | | |
| | | | |
| | | | |
| | | | |
| | | | |

# Decklist

Deck name: _____

| Number in Deck | Name | Type | Landscape |
|---|---|---|---|
| | | | |
| | | | |
| | | | |
| | | | |
| | | | |
| | | | |
| | | | |
| | | | |
| | | | |
| | | | |
| | | | |
| | | | |
| | | | |
| | | | |
| | | | |
| | | | |
| | | | |

# Decklist

Deck name: _____

| Number in Deck | Name | Type | Landscape |
|---|---|---|---|
| | | | |
| | | | |
| | | | |
| | | | |
| | | | |
| | | | |
| | | | |
| | | | |
| | | | |
| | | | |
| | | | |
| | | | |
| | | | |
| | | | |
| | | | |
| | | | |
| | | | |
| | | | |
| | | | |

# OTHER COOL CARDS

The For the Glory! Booster Pack is full of other sweet cards you can use to enhance your deck. Some of them work best in decks with a very specific goal.

**Ethan Allfire:** Talk about card advantage! If you're the Cool Guy, it's a good turn-one play because you don't mind if he gets attacked, but be careful because it can allow your opponent to ignore the Lane he is in. For a good turn-one combo, play with Blood Fortress. He's a bad attacker by himself, so use him to soak up Damage early in the game and then draw cards.

**Tip:** What if he was a 1-Action Spell that said "draw four cards"? Amazing, right? You can replace him immediately after playing him and draw your cards. He's better early before your opponent can mess with your Cornfield Landscapes.

**Sun King:** Here comes the Sun King! Hail to the king, baby! Sun King makes all your Cornfield-matter Creatures better: Corn Dog, Patchy the Pumpkin, Wall of Ears, Cornataur, Husker Knight. So load up on those dudes and fight for the corny, er, glory!

**Tip:** With 8 DEF, Sun King is pretty tough, but he needs a way to boost his ATK. Try using him in a Lane with a Blood Fortress.

**Apple Bully:** Use him as insurance against Landscape-damaging effects like the dreaded Pig. And with an ATK of 3, Apple Bully is an efficient beater. Place it next to a card like Corn Ronin, who especially likes being near Cornfield Landscapes.

**Corn Bat:** Corn Bat is at its best in a deck with three or four different Landscape types, not the Cornfield-only deck featured in the Finn vs. Jake Collector's Pack. Corn Bat is still playable in that deck, but Actions are one of your most valuable (and scarce) resources. You really want more out of your Actions than dealing 1 or 2 points of Damage. Now, *4 points?!* Wow-pow! That'll take out some enemy Creatures in one hit.

**Tip:** Since Corn Bat's ability is not a Floop ability, you can use it more than once per turn. In the right deck, Corn Bat packs a real punch.

**Grape Butt:** This is what's called a removal Spell; 1 Action, 5 Damage. That'll take out small Creatures on its own and most Creatures with any Damage on them. But this Spell takes a lot of work to work. First, you straight up can't use it in a Cornfield-only deck (unless you're lucky enough to draw a Rainbow card). Then, even if you are multi-Landscape, you need to have drawn both it and another 1- or 0-Action card of a different color. Then you're practically *forced* to use this Spell and the other one on the same turn. This one belongs in an aggressive 3- or 4-Landscape-type deck, or the sideboard for hard-to-kill utility Creatures like Cottonpult.

**Ogre Braces:** This spell has the potential to save your skin if you're low on Hit Points and high on discarded cards. Unfortunately, like many Useless Swamp cards, it only really works if you draw it late in the game. If you have the bad fortune to draw Ogre Braces early on, you might be better off just discarding it to trigger another card's power. And it's no good when your card works better in the trash than in your hand!

Ogre Braces

1

**Useless Swamp Spell**

You heal 1 Hit Point for every 5 cards in your discard pile.

**The Sludger:** The Sludger is an interesting utility Creature with a sneakily complex Floop ability. The obvious use here is as a sideboard card against other Useless Swamp decks that care about the discard pile. But did you know you can also remove cards from your own pile? Why would you want to do that? Look at cards like Red Eyeling, Gray Eyebat, or Tree of Undeath, which return random cards from your discard pile to your hand. If you remove all but one card of the given type from your discard pile, you only have one random choice, you'll get what you want every time.

The Sludger

1

**Useless Swamp Creature**

FLOOP >>> Choose a card name. Remove each card with that name in target player's discard pile from the game.

1    8

**Smoldering Elder:** Smoldering Elder is a strong (3 ATK, 8 DEF) face puncher that hurts your opponent and helps your discard pile when it enters play. It is great on turn one or later. All around, it's pretty solid.

Smoldering Elder

2

**Useless Swamp Creature**

When Smoldering Elder enters play, each player discards 2 cards.

3    8

**Raise the Dead:** One of the best cards in the game. It gives you card selection (choosing the best from a bunch of options) and Action advantage (it reduces a 2-Action Creature to 1). Plus, aren't those ghostly hands super creepy? You'll knock your opponent's socks off with fear alone. You should have 3 copies in all your Useless Swamp decks.

**Lt. Mushroom:** An excellent early play against aggressive decks, play this card in a Lane with a 2 ATK Creature to ensure it will die on your opponent's turn. Losing 3 cards is huge versus Cornfield and IcyLands decks, and it ensures a strong start.

**Djini Ghost:** This Floop ability is almonds, cashews, and all kinds of nuts. It allows you to play a Spell every turn basically for free, meaning that in a Spell-heavy card-draw deck like Finn's Blue Plains deck, you can really outpace your opponent.

**Kung Fu Power:** In a deck like Finn's Blue Plains deck, with lots of Floop Creatures, this card can give you a bit of a boost, but to really get a lot out of it, you need multiple Floop Creatures of different types in play. It's better than chocolate sprinkles if you have Finn's Hero Card in play, because your Creatures can wallop an enemy Creature with the "FLOOP >>> Deal 1 Damage to target Creature" ability.

**Travelin' Wizard:** This is a hard Creature to figure out! The obvious way to use it is to put it across from your opponent's best Creature, but remember that a 3 ATK, 3 DEF isn't nothing. Keep in mind that some Creatures (like Husker Knight) will behave much differently on your side and might even die immediately!

**Pentacutie:** This might be the best turn-one play out there. It can shut down aggressive starts from IcyLands decks and others with lots of 0-cost Creatures. It loses some of its effectiveness late in the game, but it does still have purpose against decks like BMO's Useless Swamp deck and Finn's Blue Plains deck, which have a lot of 0-cost Spell synergy. A 3 ATK, 8 DEF ain't nothing, either, although you may get better mileage out of it in the sideboard.

**Blue Ogre:** The first thing to remember is that this is always a 2 ATK, 5 DEF not a 1 ATK, 5 DEF, as you will draw a card every turn. Then, if you've got card-draw Spells like Ogre Snot, or Floop abilities like Embarrassing Bard's, Blue Ogre really packs a beating. His DEF is pretty low, so you'll want to combine him with Lane-moving effects like Teleport and Dragon Claw to maximize his effectiveness. Get him to a Lane without an enemy Creature. Blue Ogre is a great build-around card capable of carrying a whole deck.

**Portal of Unsummoning:** SandyLands decks have two primary strategies. The first is to use aggressive cards to reduce your opponent to 0 Hit Points ASAP. This card is great there, because it can bounce an enemy Creature to its owner's hand and allow you to sneak your best Creature into your opponent's Hit Points!

The other strategy is to get value out of Creatures with Enters-Play effects. Portal of Unsummoning allows you to rebuy your best one. You can even rescue your most powerful Creature, remove all Damage from it, and replay it with full DEF. The versatility of this card is the best part.

**Sandasaurus Rex:** A great turn-one play, as it's likely to be a 6 ATK, 9 DEF (*whoa*)! Unfortunately, this guy doesn't do much on a crowded board, but with all the return effects in Lady Rainicorn's SandyLands deck, you can empty a couple of Lanes on your turn and ambush your opponent with some surprise Damage.

**Lady Beetle:** The high DEF on this Creature makes it an effective blocker, and the ability is powerful. Rather than sending Creatures to the discard pile, you can put them back in your hand when they're on the verge of death. This allows you to replay powerful Enters-Play effects and keep your Creatures at a higher DEF than your opponent's Creatures.

**Psychic Tempest**: A strange and powerful effect, this card allows you to reset the DEF of all your Creatures in play, as well as reuse your Enters-Play effects. This Spell is tricky to use, because removing all Creatures at once does not leave you with a lot of Actions to play more Creatures and protect your Lanes. Many SandyLands Creatures allow you to return Creatures to hand, so why would you want a spell that does JUST this without a Creature attached to it? The only ideal situation for this spell is if you have multiple cost-0 Creatures on the board.

**Golden Axe Stump**: This is a strong, aggressive card that does Damage to your opponent even when your opponent has a Creature in its Lane. Dealing 1 a turn is fine on its own, but if your opponent is trying to draw extra cards, then the Damage really starts to pile on.

**Sack of Pain**: The ability on this Creature is in line with the rest of what NiceLands Creatures are trying to do, and although 6 Damage might be hard to hit, 8 ATK makes this one of the deadliest Creatures in the whole game.

**Witch Slap:** This Spell is super conditional, as it will almost always do nothing unless your opponent is trying to draw a million cards. Put this in the sideboard if you must, but even at its best it will only be dealing a couple points of Damage, and discarding the worst cards out of a huge hand isn't going to set your opponent back too far. At a cost of 2 Actions, it's hardly ever worth it.

**Quadurai:** Now we're talking! Unlike Witch Slap, Quadurai is a Creature, and it costs 2 fewer Actions to play. It deals 2 Damage to your opponent every turn if they're trying to draw lots of cards, and that's pretty strong when you're trying to race against their card draw.

**Fountain of Tears:** While playable in any deck, it's at its best in decks like PB's NiceLands deck or Marceline's Useless Swamp/NiceLands deck that are trying to manipulate the amount of Damage on their Creatures. And unlike the creatures in those decks, this Building is likely to stick around, allowing its bonus to be used over and over again.

# HERO CARDS

Hero Cards are special cards that are bigger than normal Card Wars cards. Each one gives your deck a unique effect. You're only allowed to have one Hero Card on your side per game, and you can only use a Hero Card if your opponent has one, too.

At the start of the game, declare who your hero is and set the appropriate Hero Card beside your deck. You don't place the Hero Card on a Landscape. Its effect remains for the entirety of the game. It cannot be removed or negated.

The Hero Cards provide benefits to a number of different strategies, but a good place to start your search for the correct hero is to match each with their namesake Collector's Pack deck.

Each Hero Card has been given a report card and a final grade to help you find the right hero for your deck. Here are the criteria, on a scale from 1 to 4.

**Aggressive:** How much does this hero boost your ability to Damage your opponent?

**Combo:** Will this hero help your cards play off each other and work in harmony?

**Control:** Does this hero give you more power to control what happens in the game?

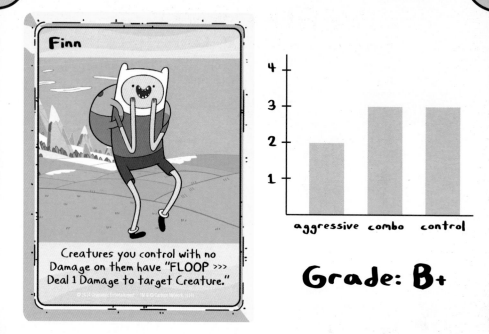

**Finn**

Creatures you control with no Damage on them have "FLOOP >>> Deal 1 Damage to target Creature."

© 2014 Cryptozoic Entertainment · TM & © Cartoon Network. (s14)

aggressive · combo · control

# Grade: B+

*You think you're gonna win? I'm gonna crush you! Party dance-style, dweeb!*

Finn's Hero Card is great if you want to control the Lanes or weaken your opponent's Creatures without getting Damage in return. To maximize the Hero Card's effect, you'll want to steadily replace your Creatures, but that will be no sweat socks because Finn's Blue Plains deck is great at drawing cards. Use your Thinking Ahead skills, and you'll be able to deploy a fresh Creature and ping an enemy Creature for the final point of Damage.

Finn's Hero Card also puts some of the cards in his Blue Plains deck into overdrive, specifically the ones that care if you have Flooped Creatures this turn (like Embarrassing Bard).

Finn's Hero Card is also strong in Lumpy Space Princess's totally lumped deck, in which replacing your Creatures with new, undamaged ones is the name of the game.

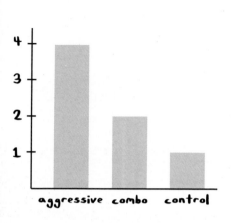

4

3

2

1

aggressive   combo   control

# Grade: C

## Jake

Creatures on facedown Landscapes
you control have +2 ATK.

© 2014 Cartoon Entertainment™   TM & © Cartoon Network (s14)

### The five winds blow through cornfields once again! For the glory of Jakoria!

Jake's Hero Card has a very specific purpose, which is to thwart one of the best counter-strategies to Jake's Cornfield deck—namely, flipping Landscapes facedown. Jake's Hero Card turns that setback into an advantage. For example, it makes several of the cards in Finn's Blue Plains deck unplayable, as they will boost you more than hurt you. It makes Husker Worm *disgustingly* powerful. Maybe you could build a deck that is all about flipping your own Landscapes to boost your Attack!

**BMO**

Discard a card from your hand >>>
Deal 1 Damage to target Creature.

© 2016 Cartoon Entertainment    TM & © Cartoon Network. (s16)

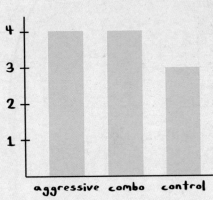

aggressive  combo  control

# Grade: A

### BMO Chop! If this were a real attack, you'd be dead.

Similar to Finn's Hero Card, BMO gives you the repeatable ability to deal 1 Damage to a Creature. "Repeatable" is key here, as it gives you a tremendous amount of flexibility in sending your opponent's Creatures to the discard pile and getting through Damage to your opponent's Hit Points.

BMO has other benefits as well. By discarding cards from your hand, you can reach that special threshold of five cards in your discard pile quickly. BMO's Hero Card has benefits in other decks as well. In decks like Princess Bubblegum's NiceLands deck and Marceline's deck, you can discard a card and Damage your own Creature to reach a Damage threshold to power up your Creature. This versatility makes BMO one of the best Hero Cards in the game.

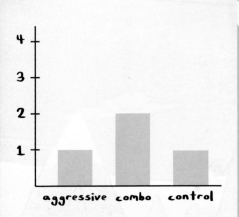

## Lady Rainicorn

If you return two or more Creatures to your hand from play or your discard pile during your turn, heal 2 HP.

© 2014 Cryptozoic Entertainment    TM & © Cartoon Network (s14)

4

3

2

1

aggressive  combo  control

# Grade: F

*<Are you joking? You are not even worth my Lady's disdain.>*

Lady Rainicorn's Hero Card lets you gain life whenever you return two or more Creatures to your hand from play or your discard pile. Lady Rainicorn's SandyLands deck is designed to repeatedly return Creatures to your hand, so if everything is going perfectly, you may gain 6-8 Hit Points over the course of a game. There are a variety of Spells and effects that return Creatures from your discard pile to your hand. Ultimately, you have to ask yourself, are the hoops you are jumping through worth the few Hit Points? The answer is—probably not. You should be more focused on playing Creatures and getting in the way of your opponent's Creatures. You'll gain way more Hit Points in the long run that way, because you won't lose them in the first place.

Sorry, Lady.

## Princess Bubblegum

Once per turn, you may deal 1 Damage to one of your Creatures. That Creature has +1 ATK this turn.

©2014 Cartoon Entertainment   TM & © Cartoon Network (s14)

**Grade: A-**

*You think we're intellectual equals? It only took me seconds to get you off your guard!*

Princess Bubblegum's Hero Card is a successful enabler for her NiceLands deck. Ultimately, the goal of that deck is to Fight your opponent's Creatures, win, and take over the game, while at the same time getting the right amount of Damage on your Creatures to power them up. It works just as well in Marceline's deck, which has similar combos. You don't need NiceLands Creatures, though. Princess Bubblegum's Hero Card is strong in a super-aggressive deck like Jake's Cornfield deck or Ice King's IcyLands deck. Don't let the 1 Damage scare you. +1 ATK is BIG GAME.

Remember, the card says you "may" deal 1 Damage. If your Creatures have too much Damage, you don't *have* to use the ability.

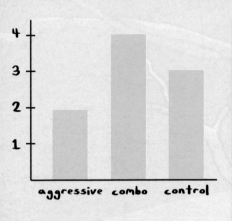

aggressive  combo  control

Grade: **B+**

Lumpy Space Princess

The first time you replace a Creature on your turn, draw a card.

© 2014 Cryptozoic Entertainment    ™ & © Cartoon Network. (s14)

## Get the **LUMP** outta here!

In Card Wars, drawing more cards than your opponent can mean the difference between being the Dweeb and being the Cool Guy. Lumpy Space Princess's Hero Card gives you a big lump up on the competition. LSP's deck already wants to be replacing its Creatures, but that is card disadvantage, because you're spending a card and Actions to defend a Lane you're already defending. LSP's Hero Card replaces the Creature you play by drawing another card into your hand. It only works once per turn, but it is still a way to make your Creatures stronger than your opponent's and keep your hand full at the same time.

**Ice King**

The first time a Creature you control attacks down an empty Lane during each of your turns, it has +1 ATK.

© 2014 Cryptozoic Entertainment    TM & © Cartoon Network (s14)

**Grade: C+**

*I have powers, too, you butts! Nyaah!*
*Ice sword! Ice shield!*

Ice King may not seem like much of a hero, but he still gets a Hero Card. He goes great in Ice King's IcyLands deck, which rewards you for attacking down empty Lanes. +1 ATK is great for an aggressive deck, and in an all-in deck that is trying to reduce an opponent's Hit Points as fast as possible, you will frequently accomplish the goal of attacking down an empty Lane. Make sure your deck has the ability to Attack down empty Lanes, whether through the Teleport Spell, Frozen Tokens, or cards that return your opponent's cards to their hand.

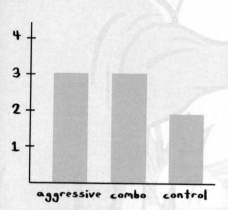

**Marceline**

Your Creatures with 5 or more Damage on them have +1 ATK.

© 2014 Cryptozoic Entertainment   TM & © Cartoon Network. (s14)

# Grade: B+

*I don't wanna hurt you. But you should know things get crazy when I'm hungry.*

In a deck like Marceline's from the Ice King vs. Marceline Collector's Pack, the Marceline Hero Card can give an extra kick to the NiceLands Creatures that get stronger when they have several points of Damage on them. Like Marceline herself, the Creatures in this deck want to tussle in a Fight, so the +1 ATK will make a big difference.

While the NiceLands synergies are nice, they are not necessary to have the Marceline Hero Card be good. Any deck with lots of Creatures will benefit from the extra +1 ATK, but is probably not at its best in a SandyLands deck or Lumpy Space Princess's deck.

**Abracadaniel**

Pay 1 Action >>> Reveal the top card of your deck. If it's a Rainbow card, play it.

© 2014 Cartoon Entertainment ™ & © Cartoon Network (s14)

**Grade: D**
(or B+, but only in an all-Rainbow deck)

aggressive   combo   control

**Maybe this is a test from destiny, guys! If we all just surrender to these events, the answer will reveal itself.**

Obviously, Abracadaniel wants to be played with a deck that is mostly, if not entirely, Rainbow cards. You score big if you pay 1 Action, reveal a Rainbow card that costs 2 Actions to play, and get to put that card into play for free. You're still up an Action if it's a Rainbow card that costs 1 Action to play.

Here's the problem. It doesn't say, "Draw the top card of your deck." It says, "Reveal." That means that if it's not a Rainbow card, you don't put it into your hand, you leave it on top of your deck, sitting there, cruelly taunting you. Now your opponent knows what card you're drawing next turn and you've wasted an Action. This is catastrophic. Honestly, spilling a tuna sandwich all over your Landscapes might be a better way to spend time during a game of Card Wars.

The other drawback is that you have to play the Rainbow card you reveal, whether you want to or not. You might waste a Spell or replace a Creature that still has all its Hit Points. Use at your own risk.

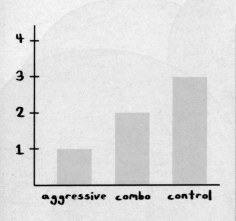

**Billy**

If your opponent's deck runs out of cards, you win the game.

©2014 Cryptozoic Entertainment. TM & © Cartoon Network. (s14)

## Grade: C-

**All my life, I've beaten on evil creatures. But new evil keeps popping up!**

In a normal game of Card Wars, when you can't draw cards from the top of your deck, you don't lose, you just have to make do with what you have. In long games that draw your whole deck, decks that can return cards from your discard pile to hand are favored. The same decks will benefit from the Billy Hero Card. In an aggressive deck, this card does nothing, as you'll want the game over before your opponent draws too many cards.

If you want to build a deck around the Billy Hero Card, check out the Blue/Corn Deck Draw custom deck in this guide.

## Cosmic Owl

Pay 1 Action >>> Look at the top 4 cards of your deck and rearrange them.

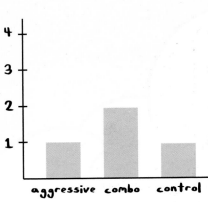

## Grade: F

*Sorry, fellas, I gotta go make some dreams come true.*

So here's a question. Let's say you use Cosmic Owl Hero Card's ability and find a card in your top 4 that you *really* don't want to draw. What happens? You can put it on the bottom of your 4-card stack, but sooner or later, you're going to draw that stinky card, anyway. That's the problem with an ability like this one. You're spending precious Actions and not gaining card advantage over your opponent.

You could combine the Cosmic Owl Hero Card with a card like Wandering Bald Man, which puts the top card of your deck into your discard pile at the beginning of your turn. You could use Cosmic Owl's ability, put a card you don't want on top of your deck, then flip it into your discard pile with Wandering Bald Man's ability on your next turn. That . . . is a lot of work for very little effect. And what the heck kinda card are you putting in your deck that you don't want to draw, anyway?

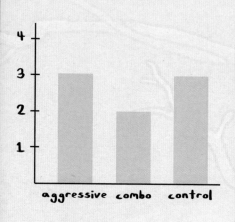

Grade: B

Huntress Wizard

At the start of the game, choose a word with 3 or more letters. Whenever you play a card with that word in its name, deal 1 Damage to target Creature an opponent controls.

© 2014 Cartoon Network. TM & © Cartoon Network. (s17)

## What's it look like, ya donk?

Here's a fun challenge: What word appears on more cards than any other? In the Collector's Packs there are a few that pop up a lot. In Princess Bubblegum's NiceLands deck alone, there's "Pie," "Eye," and "Angel." In other decks, "Sand" and "Corn" are good word choices, as you can imagine. If you're running a deck built around Slimey Creatures, with three or four different types of Landscapes, choosing "Slimey" can make all your Creatures deal 1 Damage when they enter play.

To maximize the power of the Huntress Wizard Hero Card, you have to severely restrict what cards you put in your deck. You'll have to do extensive testing to determine if putting cards in your deck that are potentially weaker is worth the benefit of the Hero Card.

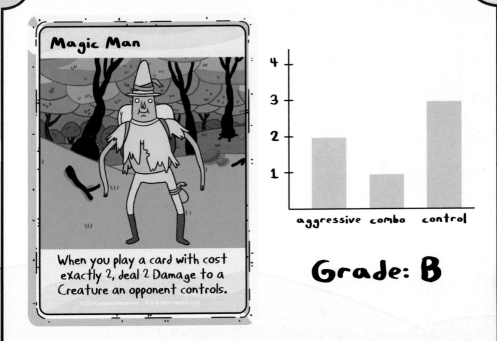

**Magic Man**

When you play a card with cost exactly 2, deal 2 Damage to a Creature an opponent controls.

Grade: **B**

## I win again, just like always!

Like most of the Hero Cards that allow certain Creatures to deal Damage to your opponent's Creatures when they enter play, the Magic Man Hero Card is good in a certain kind of deck, but the restriction can be a real liability. An overabundance of Creatures that cost 2 Actions to play may give you trouble controlling all four Lanes. If your opponent has an aggressive start, you might not be able to put Creatures in the way of each threat. Dealing 2 Damage to a Creature is a powerful effect, equal to a full card in the case of Full Metal Racket. But 2 Damage to a Creature once per turn may not be enough to change a game you are losing into a game you can win.

The Hero Card you choose doesn't have to have a game-breaking effect. A deck with a balance of 0-, 1-, and 2-Action Creatures can still get good value out of the Magic Man Hero Card, just not as much as someone running a deck that really builds around it.

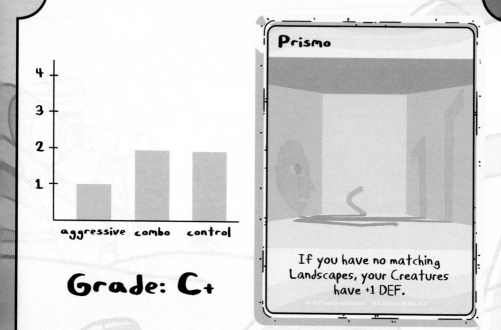

**Prismo**

If you have no matching Landscapes, your Creatures have +1 DEF.

© 2024 Cryptozoic Entertainment    TM & © Cartoon Network. (s24)

# Grade: C+

## Look, I like you, so you should know my wishes always got an ironic twist to them.

Playing with four nonmatching Landscapes is a viable deck strategy, and the Prismo Hero Card gives that deck a little boost. You will need to construct a deck of this archetype if you wish for your Creatures to gain Prismo's bonus, as any other deck simply can't use it. The main characters' decks have a limited amount of cards that work with this strategy, so you'll want to comb through the Booster Pack to find the best cards. If you can get at least one Slimey Creature for each of your Landscape types, you'll be off to a good start.

Decks with no matching Landscapes cannot play Creatures that cost 2 Actions, and the +1 DEF will give your cheap 0- and 1-Action Creatures more value. Unfortunately, +1 DEF is not as good as +1 ATK, so you will have to decide if the Prismo Hero Card is even worth it.

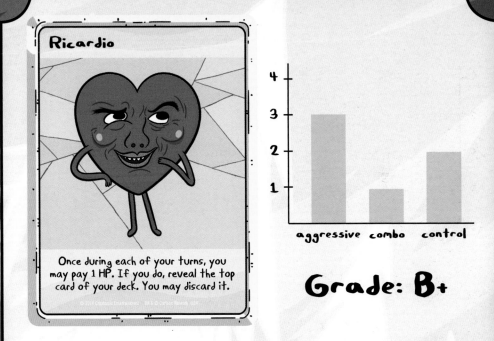

### Ricardio

Once during each of your turns, you may pay 1 HP. If you do, reveal the top card of your deck. You may discard it.

© 2016 Cartoon Network    TM & © Cartoon Network (s16)

Grade: **B+**

## One step closer and I'll remove her heart!

Oh my! Your opponent will be saying, "Stop hitting yourself," after you have spent several Hit Points on Ricardio's ability. Don't be frightened of taking Damage from Ricardio. Remember that your Hit Points are a resource that can be spent. If you are playing a Useless Swamp deck or another deck that likes discards, Ricardio's value will become apparent. Unlike other Hero Cards that mess with the top of your deck (Abracadaniel and Cosmic Owl), with this one, you can actually remove a card that you do not want to draw. Ricardio can dig to the powerful Spell or Creature you need.

There is no set time when you can use the ability, so Ricardio becomes even better if you have draw effects like Embarrassing Bard. Knowing what the top card of your deck is can confirm if you want to Floop to draw an extra card or just play what's in your hand. Just keep in mind that your opponent will see the card when you reveal it, so if you decide to leave it on top or draw it, your opponent can use that knowledge to their advantage.

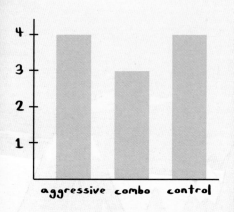

4
3
2
1

aggressive  combo  control

## Grade: A

### Susan Strong

Pay 1 Action & destroy a Creature you control >>> Deal Damage equal to its cost to each opposing Creature.

© 2018 Cartoon Network. TM & © Cartoon Network. (s18)

### Susan scared. But Susan strong!
### SUUU-SAAAAN!

Holy beans! Dealing 1–2 Damage to EACH Creature your opponent controls is mondo powerful. You can even use the ability twice in one turn and deal up to 4 Damage. That is downright apocalyptic.

The Susan Strong Hero Card is a great way to get extra value from weakened Creatures. If you can spare the Action, you should always use Susan Strong's ability instead of replacing a Creature. This makes it an anti-combo with LSP's deck, which cares about replacing Creatures on a Landscape.

One of the hidden benefits of the Susan Strong Hero Card is the threat of use. Every turn your opponent has to wonder, "What if my totally handsome opponent uses Susan Strong's ability?" If they don't plan ahead, they run the risk of having you send all their Creatures to the discard pile and dealing tons of Hit Point Damage. If they *do* play around it, then they will be losing value off the Creatures in play by replacing them early.

**Tree Trunks**

Once during each of your turns, you may discard a card with "Pie" in its name to gain 1 Action.

© 2014 Cryptozoic Entertainment · TM & © Cartoon Network (s14)

**Grade: D**

### Shoo fly, get off my apple pie!

Gaining Actions is strong, and the Tree Trunks Hero Card basically reverses the ability all players have to spend 1 Action to draw a card. But how many cards in the game even have the word "Pie" in their names? The answer is 4, so at the very most you'll be able to discard 12 cards from your deck and gain 12 Actions, assuming your deck contains the maximum number of 3 copies of each. Maybe more "Pie" cards will come out in future Card Wars expansions, but for now this ability is narrow.

Now who wants pie?

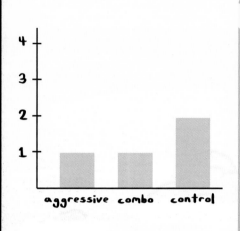

Grade: F

Lemongrab

At the start of your Fight Phase, if you have 1 or more empty Landscapes, gain 1 HP. (Can't go over 25.)

## Lemon children! Go forth! Go forth now!

The Lemongrab Hero Card allows you to gain 1 Hit Point per turn if you have a Landscape with no Creatures in it. In a deck like Lemongrab's or Lady Rainicorn's, which have SandyLands, you may be returning Creatures to your hand, leaving empty Landscapes behind. If your Landscapes are empty, 1 Hit Point won't do much to blunt your opponent's Attack. At best, Lemongrab's hero ability is a consolation for those situations where you are forced to leave an empty Landscape on the board. However, much like Lady Rainicorn's Hero Card, pure Hit Point gain won't change the outcome of a game, and you're better off choosing a more impactful Hero Card.

**Gunter**

Creatures you control on Landscapes with Frozen tokens have +1 ATK.

© 2015 Cryptozoic Entertainment. TM & © Cartoon Network. (s15)

**Grade: C+**

aggressive combo control

## Wenk! Wenk! WENNNNK!

The Gunter Hero Card has its uses. In a deck that wants to Freeze Landscapes all over the place, like Gunter's deck, Gunter can give your Creatures an ATK boost. It can also come in handy against the Ice King's deck. If your Landscapes get Frozen, you get a little extra ATK as a consolation prize, which might discourage your opponent from Freezing you as often. For the most part, Gunter's hero power is best used in combination with Creatures who like being Frozen, anyway. If you are less focused on combos, then you may be better off with the Ice King Hero Card or the Finn Hero Card.

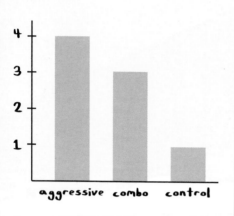

## Fionna

While you control only one Landscape type, your Rainbow Creatures have +1 ATK.

© 2016 Cryptozoic Entertainment    TM & © Cartoon Network. (s16)

## Grade: B+

### I'm gonna kick your butt! Not that I'm thinking of butts.

Rainbow Creatures don't care what your Landscape types are, so it's easy to have the Landscapes all be the same. If you do this, Fionna's Hero Card will give all your Rainbow Creatures +1 ATK. Remember, in a deck that uses Fionna, pretty much every Creature in your deck should be a Rainbow Creature. She works best in Fionna's Blue Plains deck, but maybe you can come up with a different strategy.

**Cake**

Each time a Building enters play under your control, heal 2 Damage from each Creature you control with a Building on its Landscape.

© 2016 Cartoon Entertainment · TM & © Cartoon Network (s16)

aggressive  combo  control

### Grade: B-

## My tail is totally frizzing out!

Cake's Hero Card helps give your Creatures some extra staying power. In a deck like Cake's Cornfield deck, the increased number of Buildings means your Creatures will have an easier time outlasting your opponent's Creatures, and that's good news for a deck that wants the game to go long. Remember, the ability says to heal 2 Damage from each Creature you control with a Building on its Landscape, including the Creature on the Landscape with the Building that you just played.

# JAKE'S COOL GUY GUIDE TO SIDEBOARDING

Hey, Cool Guys, Jake again, back to show you how to sideboard like a side boss. Sideboarding is an advanced technique that allows you to be more competitive against some of your deck's tougher matchups without bogging down your deck with cards that only work in special situations.

So what is a sideboard? A **sideboard** is a collection of 10 cards that you keep separate from your deck. Between games, you can swap out cards in your deck for cards in your sideboard, to improve your deck's performance. Any card legal in Card Wars is legal in a sideboard, but sideboards follow the same rules as decks. You can't have a card that costs more Actions to play than you have Landscapes of that card's type. You can't have more than 3 copies of any 1 card in your deck at a time. But you could, for example, have 2 copies of a card in your deck and a third copy in your sideboard.

**Now remember, kiddos, follow the Sideboard Commandments.**

## THOU SHALT NOT SIDEBOARD TOO MUCH.

Remember, for each card you put into your deck from the sideboard, you should take another card out. If you take out too many, you will lose too many of your deck's synergies, and the wheels will fall off the bus. DON'T LET THE WHEELS FALL OFF THE BUS! I LOVE THE BUS! Think of sideboarding like adding spice to a meal, not a side dish.

# THOU SHALT NOT SIDEBOARD TOO LOPSIDEDLY.

There's an instinct, after losing to a powerful deck, to go, "No way, Jose, I ain't gonna lose to *that* deck ever again," and then build an entire sideboard around fighting the deck that beat you. The problem is, you won't always be playing against that deck, and you never want to bring in all 10 cards from your sideboard (see Commandment #1).

# THOU SHALT BUILD A VERSATILE SIDEBOARD.

When you choose which cards to put in your sideboard, think about cards that are good against multiple types of decks. Let's say you're playing my Cornfield deck and you want to build a sideboard. What would you include? Well, a lot of decks play Buildings that are hard to get rid of, so I might put an extra copy of **Archer Dan** and 2 copies of **Volcano** in my sideboard. Then I'll add 2 copies of **The Pig** to combat other Cornfield decks (and to a lesser extent, 3- and 4-Landscape decks). Anticipating that my opponents will have anti-Cornfield cards in their sideboards, I'll include 1 **Apple Bully** and 2 **Reclaim Landscape Spells**. That'll keep my Cornfield Landscapes faceup! With my last two slots, I'll play a couple copies of **Davey Bones**, because Lady Rainicorn's SandyLands deck has been giving me trouble with aggressive starts lately.

And that's it! If you're looking for inspiration, the next few pages have some cards that should really only ever be in sideboards. Check 'em out. And happy sideboarding!

# Sideboarding Inspiration Gallery

**2** Archer Dan

**Cornfield Creature**

FLOOP >>> Destroy target Building in Archer Dan's Lane.

**2** **6**

**1** Volcano

**Rainbow Spell**

Destroy target Building in that Lane. You may deal 3 Damage to a Creature in that Lane. Flip your Landscape in that Lane face down.

**1** The Pig

**Rainbow Creature**

FLOOP >>> Flip target Cornfield Landscape in this Lane face down.

**1** **4**

**2** Apple Bully

**Cornfield Creature**

Apple Bully's Landscape cannot be flipped down by effects opponents control.

**3** **8**

**0** Reclaim Landscape

**Rainbow Spell**

You may flip one of your Landscapes face up, and you may move one of your Buildings to one of your Lanes without one.

**1** Blue Gnome

**Blue Plains Creature**

FLOOP >>> Deal 1 Damage to each opposing Creature that is on a Useless Swamp Landscape.

**1** **6**

**1** Yellow Gnome

**Cornfield Creature**

FLOOP >>> Deal 1 Damage to each opposing Creature that is on a NiceLands Landscape.

**1** **6**

**1** Life Beater Gnome

**NiceLands Creature**

FLOOP >>> Deal 1 Damage to each opposing Creature that is on a SandyLands Landscape.

**1** **6**

**1** Green Gnome

**SandyLands Creature**

FLOOP >>> Deal 1 Damage to each opposing Creature that is on a Blue Plains Landscape.

**1** **6**

**1** Fancy Pants Gnome

**Useless Swamp Creature**

FLOOP >>> Deal 1 Damage to each opposing Creature that is on a Cornfield Landscape.

**1** **6**

**1** Popcorn Power

**Cornfield Spell**

Each of your Creatures has +2 ATK this turn while attacking a Creature that is on a Blue Plains Landscape.

**1** Husker Amulet

**Cornfield Spell**

Each of your Creatures has +2 ATK this turn while attacking a Creature that is on a NiceLands Landscape.

**1** Magic Lamp

**Useless Swamp Spell**

Each of your Creatures has +2 ATK this turn while attacking a Creature that is on a SandyLands Landscape.

**1** Scroll of Bad Breath

**Useless Swamp Spell**

Each of your Creatures has +2 ATK this turn while attacking a Creature that is on a NiceLands Landscape.

**1** Scroll of Fresh Breath

**NiceLands Spell**

Each of your Creatures has +2 ATK this turn while attacking a Creature that is on a Useless Swamp Landscape.

**1** Confectionary Ring

**NiceLands Spell**

Each of your Creatures has +2 ATK this turn while attacking a Creature that is on a Cornfield Landscape.

**Snake Eyes**

1

**SandyLands Spell**

Each of your Creatures has +2 ATK
this turn while attacking a Creature
that is on a Useless Swamp Landscape.

**Lucky Penny**

1

**SandyLands Spell**

Each of your Creatures has +2 ATK
this turn while attacking a Creature
that is on a Blue Plains Landscape.

**Pink Candy**

1

**Blue Plains Spell**

Each of your Creatures has +2 ATK
this turn while attacking a Creature
that is on a SandyLands Landscape.

**Ring of Third Eye**

1

**Blue Plains Spell**

Each of your Creatures has +2 ATK
this turn while attacking a Creature
that is on a Cornfield Landscape.

**Ghost**

0

**Rainbow Creature**

Ghost has +2 ATK while defending
against a Creature that is on a
Useless Swamp Landscape.

1 / 4

**Ghost Tree**

0

**Rainbow Creature**

Ghost Tree has +2 ATK while
defending against a Creature
that is on a Cornfield Landscape.

1 / 4

**Ghost Hag**

0

**Rainbow Creature**

Ghost Hag has +2 ATK while
defending against a Creature
that is on a Blue Plains Landscape.

1 / 4

**Davey Bones**

0

**Rainbow Creature**

Davey Bones has +2 ATK while
defending against a Creature
that is on a SandyLands Landscape.

1 / 4

**Sea Hag**

2

**Rainbow Creature**

Sea Hag has +1 ATK while
attacking a Creature that is on
a Useless Swamp Landscape.

3 / 6

**Well-Dressed Wolf**

2

**Rainbow Creature**

Well-Dressed Wolf has +1 ATK while
attacking a Creature that is on a
Cornfield Landscape.

3 / 6

**Timmy Magic Eyes**

2

**Rainbow Creature**

Timmy Magic Eyes has +1 ATK
while attacking a Creature that is
on a Blue Plains Landscape.

3 / 6

**Rocktopus**

2

**Rainbow Creature**

Rocktopus has +1 ATK while
attacking a Creature that is on
a SandyLands Landscape.

3 / 6

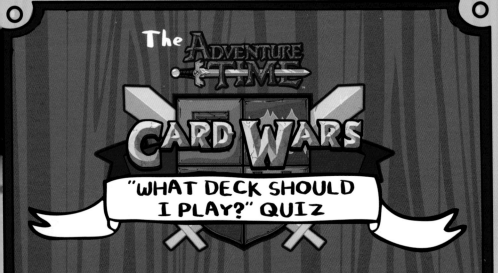

The Adventure Time

CARD WARS

## "WHAT DECK SHOULD I PLAY?" QUIZ

*If you're having trouble deciding which Landscape(s) to use, take this handy quiz!*

### Q) How do you like to fight?

1. CHAAAAAARGE!!!!
2. I don't attack until someone attacks me.
3. I dodge my enemy's attacks and go right for the heart!
4. I'd rather avoid fighting.
5. Leave me alone, I'm trying to work!
6. I'm a pacifist. Please don't hurt me. Not in the face! AH!!

### Q) How do you feel about casting arcane spells?

1. Do the spells punch my opponent in the face?
2. I only like spells if they heal my friends.
3. I will use spells to take control of the world!
4. I can be persuaded to use spells . . . maybe.
5. Spells are my favorite plaything.
6. Spells are my only friend.

## Q) What's your ideal place to live?

1. Down on a farm, shucking
2. In a gingerbread house
3. In a palace of ice, high on a frigid mountain
4. In an ancient pyramid in the desert
5. A bog, a fen, or a sludge puddle
6. On a vast prairie surrounded by magical little critters

## Q) What is a winning strategy?

1. Attack early and often, then throw mud in their eyes!
2. Carefully craft your battle plan, make slight adjustments, and then strike when the enemy least expects it.
3. Avoid the enemy's defenses and go for their weak spot.
4. Push your enemy out of the way and press on!
5. Create a 437-part plan and read it aloud to your opponent until you bore him to death.
6. Stand perfectly still and let your enemy punch you in the head until they get tired, fall down, and pass out. Then stand on top of them triumphantly!

## Q) What is your ideal pet?

1. A cute dog made out of corn stalks
2. A talking wall made out of chocolate
3. An icy dragon that breathes frost
4. A lonely Golem made of stone
5. A purple ball with arms and feet and, like, six mouths growing out of it
6. The Pig

**Q) Who do you call on when you need help?**

1. A pumpkin with an eye patch and a huge knife
2. A beautiful angel made out of vanilla ice cream
3. A living evergreen tree . . . or maybe a penguin
4. I want my mummy! . . . wrapped in bandages
5. A skeleton doctor who does more harm than good
6. A tribe of Woadic warriors, or maybe a librarian

**Q) If you could sum up the deck you want in one word, it would be _____.**

1. Attack
2. Defense
3. Cool
4. Hot
5. Discard
6. Draw card (That's two words; dang, that's five words.)

Now that you have completed the quiz, tally up the total number of times you selected each number. Whichever number you chose the most is your number, and it matches a number upside down at the bottom of this page. Whichever Landscape matches your number, that's the Landscape you should choose! If two or more numbers are tied, use a mixed deck, or try building a Rainbow deck with the numbers you chose the most!

1. Cornfield, 2. NiceLands, 3. IcyLands, 4. SandyLands, 5. Useless Swamp, 6. Blue Plains

# GLOSSARY

**Ability**—A general term for a card's special power

**Action**—Actions are the moves that you play during your turn. A card's Action cost is in the upper left corner. You can spend Actions by playing cards, drawing cards, or using special abilities on cards.

**Adjacent**—If a card triggers an effect in "an adjacent Lane," it means either of the Lanes directly next to it on your side of the game board only.

**Attack**—This is the amount of Damage a Creature is able to deal to its opponent while Fighting. If a Creature has an ability that prevents it from being "Attacked," it can still receive Damage in other ways.

**Building**—A type of card that is played below a player's Landscape card, rather than on top of it, Buildings cannot be destroyed in a Fight, and can only be removed with cards that allow a player to destroy a Building.

**Combo**—A type of strategic move that involves playing 1 card in order to maximize the benefit of another card

**Control**—A player controls the cards that are on their side of the game board

**Creature**—The soldiers of Card Wars, Creature cards must be played on empty Landscapes in order to Floop or Fight. The word *Creature* must appear on the card for it to be considered a Creature.

**Damage**—The term *Damage* applies to both Creatures and Players. Damage against a Creature impacts its Defense. Damage against a Player impacts their Hit Points.

**Defense**—The amount of Damage a Creature can take before it is destroyed. A Creature's Defense can be temporarily increased with Buildings, Spells, Hero Cards, or other Creature's abilities. A few cards, like Sand Eyebat and Ms. Mummy, can permanently increase their Defense.

**Destroy**—To send a Creature or Building to the discard pile during a Fight, with a Spell, or through another card ability

**Discard**—To put a card from your hand directly into the discard pile

**Enabler**—A card that triggers a situation that allows other cards (see Payoff) to use their maximum potential

**Exhausted**—The opposite of "Ready," an exhausted Creature cannot Floop or Fight until it is readied again.

**Floop**—A special ability found on some cards; a Creature that is Flooped cannot Fight.

**Freeze**—Some cards allow you to Freeze your or your opponent's Landscape. Creatures cannot be placed on a Frozen Landscape. The player who controls the Landscape must discard a card in order to remove the Frozen token.

**Hit Points**—Each player begins with 25 Hit Points. The goal is to reduce the Opponent's Hit Points to 0. Hit Points can be lost when a Creature Attacks down an empty Lane, through Spells, or through special card abilities.

**Landscape**—The game board is made up of 8 Landscape cards, 4 on each player's side. The types of Landscapes on the board determine which cards can be played.

**Lane**—There are 4 Lanes of play on the game board. Each Lane is formed by a Landscape from both you and your opponent.

**Leave play**—When a Creature is removed from the board for any reason

**Opponent**—The other player of the game; Attacks or Abilities that deal damage to your opponent directly affect their Hit Points.

**Opposing**—If a card has an ability that targets "opposing Creatures," it means the cards that belong to your opponent.

**Payoff**—Cards whose abilities are improved by other cards (see Enabler)

**Players**—The actual people playing Card Wars

**Random**—If you are told to draw or discard a random card, you do not get to choose which one. If you are told to return a random card of a certain type to your hand from your discard, remove all cards of that type from the discard, shuffle them together, and choose one without looking.

**Ready**—A card in the Ready position is able to Fight, Floop, or use other abilities. Each player readies all their cards at the beginning of their turn.

**Replace**—To remove one card (usually a Creature) from the board, and put another in its place. You do not need to pay an Action to remove a card, but you still need to play the new card's Action cost to place it on the board.

**Reveal**—When you reveal a card, it must be shown to both players.

**Sacrifice**—To willingly destroy one of your own cards to trigger an effect

**Sideboard**—A set of cards that is separate from the main deck that players can add to their deck to customize their strategy; it is not necessary to play with a sideboard, but it can be useful when playing with custom-built decks.

**Spell**—A card with a one-time ability

**Target**—The words "target Creature" or "target Opponent" on a card mean that you can apply that card's effects to whichever Creature or Opponent you decide to target.

**Utility**—A utility card is one that has a simple, straightforward effect, and is useful in a wide variety of deck strategies.

# CARD LIST

**Abdominal Snowman**
IcyLands Creature
+3 ATK while your opponent does not control a Creature in this Lane.
1 · 3🔨 · 2🛡

**Abraca Amadeus**
Useless Swamp Spell
Target opponent discards a card from his hand for every 5 cards in your discard pile.
2

**Albino Eyebat**
NiceLands Creature
While Albino Eyebat has exactly 2 Damage on it, it has +2 ATK.
1 · 2🔨 · 7🛡

**Amazing Avalanche**
Cornfield Spell
Each of your Creatures has +1 ATK this turn for each face-down Landscape in play.
1

**Ancient Scholar**
Blue Plains Creature
FLOOP >>> Return a random Rainbow card from your discard pile to your hand. If you control a Building in this Lane, gain 1 Action.
1 · 1🔨 · 7🛡

**Angel Heart**
Rainbow Creature
While Angel Heart has exactly 2 Damage on it, it has +3 ATK.
0 · 0🔨 · 7🛡

**Angel of Chocolate**
NiceLands Creature
Pay 1 Action >>> Heal all Damage from Angel of Chocolate.
2 · 3🔨 · 7🛡

**Angel of Vanilla**
NiceLands Creature
Pay 1 Action >>> Heal all Damage from Angel of Vanilla.
1 · 2🔨 · 6🛡

**Apple Bully**
Cornfield Creature
Apple Bully's Landscape cannot be flipped down by effects opponents control.
2 · 3🔨 · 8🛡

**Apple Pieclops**
NiceLands Creature
At the start of your turn, you may heal or deal 1 Damage to each Creature you control. (Choose for each Creature.)
2 · 1🔨 · 7🛡

**Archer Dan**
Cornfield Creature
FLOOP >>> Destroy target Building in Archer Dan's Lane.
2 · 2🔨 · 6🛡

**Archer Danica**
Cornfield Creature
Destroy a Building you control and Floop >>> Deal 3 Damage to each opposing Creature.
2 · 1🔨 · 6🛡

**Auto-Plucker**
NiceLands Building
FLOOP >>> Heal or Deal 1 Damage to your Creature in this Lane.
1

**Ban-She Princess**
Useless Swamp Creature
When Ban She Princess enters play, you may remove a token from an adjacent Landscape.
1 · 2🔨 · 7🛡

**Ban-She Queen**
Useless Swamp Creature
When Ban She Queen enters play, you may remove a token from an adjacent Landscape.
2 · 3🔨 · 9🛡

**Beach Mummy**
SandyLands Creature
FLOOP >>> Return a Creature in an adjacent Lane to its owner's hand.
1 · 1🔨 · 6🛡

**Big Foot**
Rainbow Creature
FLOOP >>> Flip target face-down Landscape you control face up.
0 · 1🔨 · 4🛡

**The Big Hen House**
NiceLands Building
At the start of your turn, deal 1 or 2 Damage to your Creature in this Lane, then you heal 1 HP (Max 25).
1

**Black Hole Pendant**
Rainbow Spell
Target Creature has +X ATK this turn, where X is the number of different Landscape types your opponent controls.
0

**Black Paladin**
Useless Swamp Creature
+1 ATK for each card players (including you) have discarded from their hand this turn.
1 · 1🔨 · 7🛡

**Blonde MerWitch** — 2

*Rainbow Creature*

The seas are her cauldron, and her ingredients are anything that sinks.

3 / 9

**Blood Bath** — 2

*Useless Swamp Spell*

Target foe may discard a card with cost 2 or greater. If they do not, deal 5 Damage to that foe.

**Blood Castle** — 1

*Rainbow Building*

Each time an opposing Creature in this Lane takes Damage, increase the amount by 1.

**Blood Fortress** — 1

*Rainbow Building*

Your Creature in this Lane has +1 ATK.

**Blood Transfusion** — 0

*Rainbow Spell*

Remove from game a card in any player's discard pile. Heal X Damage from target Creature, where X is the cost of the card removed this way.

**Blueberry Djini** — 1

*Blue Plains Creature*

When Blueberry Djini enters play, if it replaced a Creature, draw two cards.

2 / 6

**Blueberry Pieclops** — 4

*Blue Plains Creature*

Blueberry Pieclops costs 1 less to play for each Spell you have played this turn.

5 / 6

**Blue Candy** — 1

*NiceLands Spell*

Heal up to 7 Damage from target Creature you control.

**Blue Gnome** — 1

*Blue Plains Creature*

FLOOP >>> Deal 1 Damage to each opposing Creature that is on a Useless Swamp Landscape.

1 / 6

**Blue Merlock** — 1

*Useless Swamp Creature*

FLOOP >>> Draw a card, and then discard a card.

2 / 5

**Blue Ogre** — 2

*Blue Plains Creature*

Whenever you draw a card, Blue Ogre has +1 ATK this turn.

1 / 5

**Blue Slimey** — 1

*Blue Plains Creature*

If you control 3 or more different Landscape types when Blue Slimey enters play, return a Creature in this Lane to its owner's hand.

2 / 6

**Boarder Collie** — 1

*IcyLands Creature*

FLOOP >>> Move Boarder Collie to any of your empty Landscapes. If either Landscape in that Lane is Frozen, gain 1 Action.

1 / 7

**Bog Ban-She Angel** — 2

*Useless Swamp Creature*

Pay 1 Action >>> Move all Damage on this Creature to target Creature.

2 / 7

**Bog Bum** — 1

*Useless Swamp Creature*

If Bog Bum leaves play while Ready, each opponent discards a random card.

2 / 6

**Bog Frog Bomb** — 2

*Useless Swamp Creature*

If Bog Frog Bomb leaves play while Ready, deal 2 Damage to each opposing Creature.

3 / 8

**Bone Wand** — 0

*Rainbow Spell*

Play only if you control a Useless Swamp Creature. Target opponent discards a card from his hand.

**Bouncing Zebracorn** — 2

*Cornfield Creature*

+1 ATK for each different Landscape type you control.

1 / 9

**Brain Gooey** — 1

*Blue Plains Creature*

When Brain Gooey enters play, if it replaced a Creature, it has +2 ATK this turn.

1 / 7

**Brief Power** — 0

*Rainbow Spell*

Target Useless Swamp Creature you control has +2 ATK this turn.

**Business Dog** — 1

*Blue Plains Creature*

Business Dog has +2 ATK this turn for each card you have played with "Dog" or "Puppy" in its title this turn.

1 / 6

**Buns Away!** — 1

*Useless Swamp Spell*

Target foe may discard a card. If they do not, deal 2 Damage to each of their Creatures.

**Burly Lumberjack** — 2

*Cornfield Creature*

You may play additional Buildings onto this Landscape.

2 / 9

**Cabin of Many Woods** — 5

*Cornfield Building*

Cabin of Many Woods costs 1 less to play for each Flooped Creature you control.

Your Creature in this Lane has +5 DEF.

**Cactus Thug** — 1

*SandyLands Creature*

Adjacent Cornfield Creatures have +1 ATK.

2 / 7

**Captain Taco** — 1
*Cornfield Creature*
When Captain Taco enters play, deal 1 Damage to each Creature that is not on a CornField Landscape.
1 / 1

**Cardboard Mansion** — 5
*Useless Swamp Building*
Cardboard Mansion costs 1 less to play for every 5 cards in your discard pile.
FLOOP >>> Gain 1 Action.

**Carmel Camel** — 1
*SandyLands Creature*
When a Creature you own leaves play, you may put it underneath this card instead. +1 ATK and +1 DEF for each card under this. When this card leaves play, discard all cards under it.
0 / 4

**Cave of Solitude** — 2
*NiceLands Building*
Discard a card >>> Your Creature in this Lane can't be targeted or attacked until the start of your next turn.

**Celestial Castle** — 1
*Rainbow Building*
Your Creature in this Lane has +3 DEF.

**Celestial Fortress** — 1
*Rainbow Building*
The opposing Creature in this Lane has -2 DEF.

**Cerebral Bloodstorm** — 1
*Rainbow Spell*
Deal 3 Damage to each opposing Creature.

**Charming City** — 1
*Blue Plains Building*
All Creatures in this Lane lose their Landscape type and become Rainbow Creatures.

**Chest Burster** — 1
*Useless Swamp Creature*
At the start of your turn, deal 3 Damage to each opponent who has no cards in hand.
1 / 10

**Cold Soldier** — 1
*IcyLands Creature*
+2 ATK while your opponent does not control a Creature in this Lane.
2 / 4

**Confectionary Ring** — 1
*NiceLands Spell*
Each of your Creatures has +2 ATK this turn while attacking a Creature that is on a Cornfield Landscape.

**Cool Dog** — 2
*Blue Plains Creature*
Your Creatures on adjacent Lanes may not be Attacked.
2 / 7

**The Cooler** — 2
*IcyLands Creature*
When The Cooler leaves play, Freeze its Landscape.
4 / 7

**Corn Bat** — 1
*Cornfield Creature*
Pay 1 Action >>> Deal 3 Damage to target Creature in this Lane for each different Landscape type you control.
2 / 7

**Corn Dog** — 1
*Cornfield Creature*
Corn Dog has +1 DEF for each Cornfield Landscape you control. If you control 3 or fewer Cornfield Landscapes, Corn Dog has +1 ATK.
0 / 12

**Corn Lord** — 1
*Cornfield Creature*
Corn Lord has +1 ATK for each other Cornfield Creature you control.
0 / 7

**Corn Ronin** — 1
*Cornfield Creature*
+1 ATK for each adjacent Cornfield Landscape.
1 / 6

**Corn Scepter** — 1
*Rainbow Spell*
Deal 1 Damage to target Creature for each Cornfield Landscape you control.

**Cornataur** — 2
*Cornfield Creature*
When Cornataur enters play, deal 1 Damage to your opponent for each Cornfield Landscape you control.
2 / 10

**Corns Templar** — 1
*Cornfield Creature*
Floop >>> Heal 1 Damage from Corns Templar.
1 / 7

**Cotton Devil** — 2
*NiceLands Creature*
+1 DEF for each different Landscape type you control.
4 / 1

**Cotton Eyebat** — 1
*NiceLands Creature*
While Cotton Eyebat has exactly 4 Damage on it, it has +4 ATK.
1 / 8

**Cottonpult** — 1
*NiceLands Creature*
FLOOP >>> Deal 1 Damage to target Creature. If Cottonpult has 3 or more Damage on it, it heals 1 Damage and readies.
1 / 8

**Cow** — 0
*Rainbow Creature*
Moo.
1 / 5

**Cowspar** — 2
*Cornfield Creature*
Each adjacent Cornfield Creature has +1 DEF.
3 / 8

 **Crazy Cat Lady** — 2
Blue Plains Creature
Rainbow Creatures you control have +1 ATK.
1 / 10

 **Cross Pollination** — 2
Rainbow Spell
Each of your Cornfield Creatures has +1 ATK this turn for each different Landscape type you control.

 **Crystal Palace** — 1
IcyLands Building
When a Landscape in this Lane becomes Frozen, deal 7 Damage to target Creature.

 **Cute Overload** — 0
Rainbow Spell
Destroy any number of Creatures you control. Draw a card for each Creature destroyed this way.

 **Cutie** — 1
NiceLands Creature
FLOOP >>> You heal 1 Hit Point. (Can't go over 25.)
0 / 6

---

 **Dark Angel** — 1
Useless Swamp Creature
+1 ATK for every 5 cards in your discard pile.
0 / 5

 **Davey Bones** — 0
Rainbow Creature
Davey Bones has +2 ATK while defending against a Creature that is on a SandyLands Landscape.
1 / 4

 **Deforestation** — 2
Cornfield Spell
Additional Cost: Floop a Creature you control.
Search your deck for a Building and put it into play. Then shuffle your deck.

 **Diamond Dan** — 1
SandyLands Creature
When Diamond Dan leaves play from a NiceLands Landscape, return it to its owner's hand.
2 / 2

 **Djini Ghost** — 1
Blue Plains Creature
FLOOP >>> Pay 1 less to play your next Spell this turn.
1 / 6

---

 **The Dog** — 1
Rainbow Creature
Floop >>> Opposing Buildings in this Lane are blank while The Dog is Flooped.
"Woof."
1 / 7

 **Dogboy** — 0
Rainbow Creature
Discard a card >>> Dogboy has +2 ATK this turn. (Use only once during each of your turns.)
0 / 5

 **Dragon Claw** — 1
Blue Plains Creature
FLOOP >>> Move a Creature you control to an empty Lane.
1 / 8

 **Dragon Foot** — 1
Useless Swamp Creature
Discard a card >>> Dragon Foot has +1 ATK this turn. (Use up to five times during each of your turns.)
1 / 5

 **Dragon Parrotrooper** — 2
Rainbow Creature
When Dragon Parrotrooper enters play, move it to any empty Landscape. It cannot be replaced. Adjacent Creatures have -1 ATK.
1 / 8

---

 **Drained Cleric** — 1
Blue Plains Creature
At the start of your turn, move Drained Cleric to an empty Landscape you control. If you cannot, discard a card.
3 / 5

**Dr. Death** — 2
Useless Swamp Creature
Destroy a Creature you control and FLOOP >>> Destroy target opposing Creature in this Lane.
1 / 7

 **Dr. Stuffenstein** — 2
NiceLands Creature
FLOOP >>> Heal 2 Damage from a Creature on an adjacent Landscape. If Dr. Stuffenstein has 7 or more Damage on it, heal 7 Damage from each of your Creatures instead.
1 / 9

 **Drooling Dude** — 2
Rainbow Creature
The ladies love him, as long as they have waterproof shoes.
3 / 9

 **Drop Zone** — 0
Rainbow Spell
Return target Creature you own to your hand.

---

 **Druid of the Cob** — 1
Cornfield Creature
Flooped Creatures you control have +1 ATK.
1 / 8

 **Earth Mover** — 2
Cornfield Creature
+2 ATK for each face-down Landscape in play.
2 / 10

 **Elf Hut** — 1
Blue Plains Building
Pay 1 Action >>> Draw a card for each Creature in this Lane.

 **Embarrassing Bard** — 2
Blue Plains Creature
FLOOP >>> Draw a card for each Flooped Creature you control (including this one).
1 / 5

 **Emboldened Retriever** — 2
Blue Plains Creature
Each time Emboldened Retriever attacks, you may draw a card.
"Mush bah! Woo!"
2 / 7

**Emperor Penguin** — 1

IcyLands Creature

Creatures on Landscapes with a Frozen token on it have -1 ATK.

ATK 1 / DEF 8

**Ethan Allfire** — 1

Cornfield Creature

When Ethan Allfire leaves play, draw 1 card for each Cornfield Landscape you control.

ATK 0 / DEF 4

**Evil Eye** — 0

Rainbow Creature

Evil is in the eye of the beholder.

DEF 5

**Extraordinary Spider** — 1

Useless Swamp Creature

At the start of your turn, deal 1 Damage to target opponent for every 5 cards in your discard pile.

ATK 1 / DEF 7

**Eye Guy** — 1

Useless Swamp Creature

At the start of your turn, look at the top card of your deck. You may put it on the bottom of your deck.

ATK 1 / DEF 8

**Fairy Shepard** — 2

NiceLands Creature

Each adjacent NiceLands Creature has +2 DEF.

ATK 2 / DEF 9

**Falling Star** — 2

NiceLands Spell

Creatures you control take no Damage from opposing Creatures this turn.

**Fancy Pants Gnome** — 1

Useless Swamp Creature

FLOOP ••• Deal 1 Damage to each opposing Creature that is on a Cornfield Landscape.

ATK 1 / DEF 6

**Fancy Spa** — 1

Blue Plains Building

At the start of your Fight Phase, if you control an exhausted Creature on this Landscape, draw a card.

**Fancy Zebracorn** — 1

Cornfield Creature

+1 DEF for each different Landscape type you control.

ATK 2 / DEF 4

**Farmhouse** — 2

Cornfield Building

Farmhouse counts as an additional Cornfield Landscape you control.

**Fatapillar** — 2

Useless Swamp Creature

+1 ATK for every 3 cards in your discard pile.

ATK 0 / DEF 3

**Fatigued Librarian** — 1

Blue Plains Creature

Fatigued Librarian comes into play exhausted and does not ready at the start of your turn. Whenever Fatigued Librarian changes Lanes, ready it.

ATK 3 / DEF 4

**Fiddling Ferret** — 1

Blue Plains Creature

Floop >>> Draw a card, and then discard a card. If you discard a Rainbow card this way, gain 1 Action.

ATK 1 / DEF 6

**Field of Nightmares** — 1

Cornfield Spell

Deal 1 Damage to your opponent for each card in his hand.

**Field Reaper** — 1

Cornfield Creature

Additional Cost: Discard a card. When Field Reaper enters play, move target Creature in this Lane to an adjacent empty Lane on your side.

ATK 1 / DEF 4

**Field Stalker** — 1

Cornfield Creature

At the start of your turn, each player draws a card.

ATK 1 / DEF 10

**Fisher Fish** — 1

Useless Swamp Creature

If Fisher Fish enters play onto a Blue Plains Landscape, deal 1 Damage to each opposing player.

ATK 2 / DEF 6

**Floating Ice Palace** — 2

IcyLands Building

Your Creature on this Landscape has +1 ATK during your turn for each Landscape with a Frozen token on it.

**Fly Swatter** — 1

Useless Swamp Creature

FLOOP >>> Each opponent discards a card with cost 0, or reveals a hand with none.

ATK 1 / DEF 6

**Fountain of Tears** — 0

Rainbow Building

While your Creature in this Lane has exactly 3 Damage on it, it has +3 ATK.

**Free Fall** — 1

SandyLands Spell

Each of your Creatures has +1 ATK this turn for each Creature that entered play this turn.

**Freeze Ray** — 1

IcyLands Spell

Freeze target Landscape, and then draw a card.

**Freezing Point** — 2

IcyLands Spell

Freeze each of your opponent's Landscapes.

**Friendship Bracelet** — 0

Rainbow Spell

Swap any amount of Damage between two Creatures you control.

**Fright Tower** `1`

Useless Swamp Building

Pay 1 Action >>> Target Creature in this Lane has +1 ATK for every 5 cards in your discard pile.

---

**Frost Dragon** `2`

IcyLands Creature

Pay 1 Action >>> Freeze a Landscape in this Lane.

2💧 / 10❤

---

**Frosted Deanimator** `1`

IcyLands Creature

Frosted Deanimator may enter play onto a Landscape that has a Frozen token on it.

2💧 / 6❤

---

**Frosted Snowwoman** `2`

IcyLands Creature

When Frosted Snowwoman enters play, Freeze both Landscapes in her Lane.

3💧 / 5❤

---

**Frosty Frolic** `2`

IcyLands Spell

Target player discards 1 card from her hand for each Landscape with a Frozen token on it she controls.

---

**Frozen Fish** `1`

IcyLands Creature

When Frozen Fish deals Damage to a Creature, you may Freeze a Landscape in this Lane.

1💧 / 8❤

---

**Frozen Heart** `0`

Rainbow Spell

Deal 1 Damage to target Creature. If that Creature is on a Landscape with a Frozen token on it, deal 2 Damage instead.

---

**Full Metal Racket** `0`

Rainbow Spell

Deal 2 Damage to target Creature.

---

**Fummy** `1`

SandyLands Creature

FLOOP >>> Gain 1 Action this turn.

2💧 / 7❤

---

**Funeral Home** `1`

Useless Swamp Building

Whenever a foe discards a card, your Creature in this Lane has +1 ATK until end of turn.

---

**Furious Chick** `0`

Rainbow Creature

Furious Chick has +1 ATK for each Damage on it.

0💧 / 5❤

---

**Furious Furor** `1`

Cornfield Spell

Target Creature has +2 ATK this turn for each Flooped Creature you control.

---

**Furious Hen** `2`

NiceLands Creature

Furious Hen has +1 ATK for each Damage on it.

0💧 / 10❤

---

**Furious Rooster** `1`

NiceLands Creature

Furious Rooster has +1 ATK for each Damage on it.

0💧 / 8❤

---

**Future Scholar** `2`

Blue Plains Creature

When Future Scholar enters play, if it replaced a Creature, gain 1 Action.

2💧 / 8❤

---

**Ghost** `0`

Rainbow Creature

Ghost has +1 ATK while defending against a Creature that is on a Useless Swamp Landscape.

1💧 / 4❤

---

**Ghost Chest Booster** `1`

Useless Swamp Creature

When Ghost Chest Booster leaves play, draw the bottom card of your deck.

1💧 / 9❤

---

**Ghost Hag** `0`

Rainbow Creature

Ghost Hag has +2 ATK while defending against a Creature that is on a Blue Plains Landscape.

1💧 / 4❤

---

**Ghost Ninja** `1`

Blue Plains Creature

When Ghost Ninja deals Damage to an opposing player, that opponent can't play Spells during his next turn.

2💧 / 7❤

---

**Ghost Tree** `0`

Rainbow Creature

Ghost Tree has +2 ATK while defending against a Creature that is on a Cornfield Landscape.

1💧 / 4❤

---

**Giant Mummy Hand** `1`

SandyLands Creature

FLOOP >>> Deal 1 Damage to target Creature for each Cornfield Landscape adjacent to this Lane.

0💧 / 7❤

---

**Glacier Racer** `1`

IcyLands Creature

+4 ATK if both Landscapes in this Lane have Frozen tokens on them.

2💧 / 6❤

---

**Glorious Gramophone** `1`

Blue Plains Spell

Draw 4 cards, then discard 2 cards.

---

**Gnome Snot** `1`

Blue Plains Spell

Draw 3 cards.

---

**Goat** `0`

Rainbow Creature

When Goat enters play, if it replaced a Creature, draw a card.

1💧 / 4❤

---

# Row 1

**Gold Ninja** — 1
Cornfield Creature
When Gold Ninja enters play, deal 1 Damage to target Creature for each different Landscape type you control.
2 / 6

**Golden Axe Stump** — 1
SandyLands Creature
Whenever an opponent draws a card, deal 1 Damage to that player.
1 / 7

**Golden Jackal** — 1
Cornfield Creature
FLOOP and discard a SandyLands card >>> Deal 1 Damage to each opposing Creature.
1 / 4

**Grand Mummy** — 1
SandyLands Creature
At the start of your turn, you may return Grand Mummy to its owner's hand. If you do, draw two cards.
3 / 3

**Grape Butt** — 1
Cornfield Spell
Play only if you played a non-Cornfield card this turn. Deal 5 Damage to target Creature.

# Row 2

**Grape Djini** — 1
Blue Plains Creature
When Grape Djini enters play, if it replaced a Creature, you may put a card from your discard pile on top of your deck.
1 / 6

**Gray Eyebat** — 1
Useless Swamp Creature
Pay 1 Action >>> Return a random Useless Swamp Creature from your discard pile to your hand.
2 / 7

**Green Cactiball** — 1
SandyLands Creature
+2 ATK for each Green Cactiball you control.
0 / 4

**Green Candy** — 0
Rainbow Spell
Heal or deal 1 Damage to target Creature.

**Green Gnome** — 1
SandyLands Creature
FLOOP >>> Deal 1 Damage to each opposing Creature that is on a Blue Plains Landscape.
1 / 6

# Row 3

**Green Mermaid** — 1
Useless Swamp Creature
Destroy Green Mermaid >>> Deal 1 Damage to each opposing Creature.
1 / 9

**Green Merman** — 2
Useless Swamp Creature
FLOOP >>> Put the top of your deck into your discard pile. Deal damage to each opposing Creature equal to the discarded card's Action Cost.
0 / 6

**Green Party Ogre** — 1
SandyLands Creature
When a Creature you control leaves play, heal 1 Damage from Green Party Ogre.
1 / 8

**Green Snakey** — 1
SandyLands Creature
When Green Snakey leaves play, deal 1 Damage to target Creature in this Lane.
1 / 6

**Ham Fist** — 0
Rainbow Spell
Target Creature you control has +3 ATK this turn. Draw a card.

# Row 4

**Harvest Moon** — 2
Cornfield Spell
Put a Building from your discard pile into play.

**Headphone Jerk** — 2
Blue Plains Creature
When Headphone Jerk enters play, if it replaced a Creature, deal 3 Damage to another Creature in this Lane.
2 / 7

**Heavenly Gazer** — 1
Blue Plains Creature
FLOOP >>> Put a Spell from your discard pile on top of your deck.
2 / 5

**Helping Hand** — 0
Rainbow Creature
Floop >>> Return a Building from your discard pile to your hand.
1 / 4

**Herculeye** — 2
Useless Swamp Creature
Discard a card >>> Herculeye has +4 ATK this turn. (Use only once during each of your turns.)
1 / 6

# Row 5

**Hot Eyebat** — 1
Useless Swamp Creature
Play Hot Eyebat only if you have 10 or more cards in your discard pile.
4 / 4

**Hunkclops** — 1
Rainbow Creature
3 / 3

**Husker Amulet** — 1
Cornfield Spell
Each of your Creatures has +2 ATK this turn while attacking a Creature that is on a NiceLands Landscape.

**Husker Champion** — 1
Cornfield Creature
Husker Champion has +2 ATK and +2 DEF if you control a Building on this Landscape.
1 / 1

**Husker Knight** — 2
Cornfield Creature
Husker Knight has +1 ATK and +2 DEF for each Cornfield Landscape you control.
X / X

**Husker Valkyrie**
2

Cornfield Creature

Husker Valkyrie has +2 ATK and +2 DEF if you control a Building on this Landscape.

2 / 6

**Husker Worm**
1

Cornfield Creature

When Husker Worm enters play, flip a Cornfield Landscape you control face down.

5 / 4

**Husky Parratrooper**
2

Rainbow Creature

When Husky Parratrooper enters play, move it to any empty Landscape, and then flip that Landscape face down.

2 / 4

**Icemeister**
2

IcyLands Creature

At the start of your turn, deal 1 Damage to each Creature on a Landscape with a Frozen token on it.

1 / 10

**Ice-olation Cell**
1

IcyLands Building

Creatures on Landscapes with a Frozen token on it in this Lane cannot Attack or use abilities.

---

**Icy Commando**
1

IcyLands Creature

Icy Commando has +1 ATK for each Landscape with a Frozen token on it.

1 / 7

**Icy Infiltrator**
0

Rainbow Spell

When Icy Infiltrator enters play, Freeze its Landscape.

1 / 5

**Icy Intruder**
1

IcyLands Creature

Pay 1 Action, FLOOP ••• Freeze target Landscape.

1 / 8

**Igloo of Sanctuary**
1

Blue Plains Building

FLOOP ••• If your Creature in this Lane moved here from another Lane this turn it has +3 ATK this turn.

**Immortal Maize Walker**
2

Useless Swamp Creature

While Immortal Maize Walker is on a Cornfield Landscape, it deals triple Damage.

2 / 8

---

**Impossible Possum**
2

Blue Plains Creature

When this card is placed into your Discard pile from anywhere, you may discard a card from your hand to return Impossible Possum to your hand.

2 / 8

**Incredible Egg**
0

Rainbow Spell

Reveal the top 3 cards of your deck. You may put a revealed Cornfield card into your hand. Discard the rest.

**Industrial Assassin**
1

Blue Plains Creature

Destroy a Creature you control, FLOOP ••• Draw a card.

2 / 6

**Infant Scholar**
1

Blue Plains Creature

If you played one or more Rainbow cards this turn, Infant Scholar has +3 ATK this turn.

1 / 6

**Infinite Figure**
1

Useless Swamp Creature

Discard a card ••• Deal 1 Damage to another Creature in this Lane. (Use any number of times during each of your turns.)

1 / 6

---

**Jinxed Parratrooper**
1

Rainbow Creature

When Jinxed Parratrooper enters play, move it to any empty Landscape. It cannot be replaced. At the start of your turn, discard a card.

1 / 5

**Kernel Queen**
1

Cornfield Creature

Kernel Queen has +1 ATK for each Flooped Creature you control.

1 / 6

**Kung Fu Power**
1

Blue Plains Spell

Ready 1 Creature of each type you control. (The types are Cornfield, Rainbow, Useless Swamp, Blue Plains, NiceLands, and SandyLands.)

**Lady Beetle**
1

SandyLands Creature

At the start of your turn, you may return a Creature you control with 2 or fewer DEF remaining to its owner's hand.

1 / 9

**Learning Center**
2

Blue Plains Building

Learning Center gains the game text of Buildings you control in adjacent Lanes (but not their names).

---

**Legion of Earlings**
2

Cornfield Creature

When Legion of Earlings enters play, you may return target Creature in this Lane to its owner's hand.

2 / 8

**Life Beater Gnome**
1

NiceLands Creature

FLOOP ••• Deal 1 Damage to each opposing Creature that is on a SandyLands Landscape.

1 / 6

**Lime Slimey**
1

SandyLands Creature

If you control 2 or more different Landscape types when Lime Slimey enters play, draw 2 cards.

2 / 6

**Little Freezy**
2

Blue Plains Creature

+1 DEF for each different Landscape type you control.

4 / 1

**Log Knight**
1

Cornfield Creature

FLOOP ••• Put a Building from your hand below this Lane (if it doesn't already have one).

2 / 2

 **Log Rhythm** — 1
**Cornfield Spell**
Each Creature you control with a Building on its Landscape has +2 ATK this turn.

 **Lonely Panda** — 1
**Blue Plains Creature**
When Lonely Panda enters play, if you control no other Creatures, draw a card.
1 / 8

 **Lost Golem** — 3
**SandyLands Creature**
Lost Golem costs 1 less to play for each other Creature you have played this turn.
5 / 6

 **Lt. Mushroom** — 1
**Useless Swamp Creature**
When Lt. Mushroom leaves play during an opponent's turn, that opponent discards 2 cards.
2 / 3

 **Lucky Penny** — 1
**SandyLands Spell**
Each of your Creatures has +2 ATK this turn while attacking a Creature that is on a Blue Plains Landscape.

 **Lumbercaddy** — 1
**Cornfield Creature**
Floop >>> Move target Building you control to any Landscape without one.
2 / 6

 **Lunchpad** — 2
**SandyLands Building**
FLOOP >>> Draw a card for each Creature that entered play onto this Landscape this turn.

 **Mace Stump** — 1
**Useless Swamp Creature**
Destroy Mace Stump >>> Target opponent discards a card for every 5 cards in your discard pile.
3 / 3

 **Magenapping** — 2
**Blue Plains Spell**
Play only if you control one or fewer Creatures and have 15 or fewer Hit Points. Move target Creature to target empty Landscape you control.

 **Magic Lamp** — 1
**Useless Swamp Spell**
Each of your Creatures has +2 ATK this turn while attacking a Creature that is on a SandyLands Landscape.

 **Magic Ring Ding** — 2
**Useless Swamp Spell**
Each of your Creatures has +1 ATK this turn for every 5 cards in your discard pile.

 **Mantle Masher** — 2
**Cornfield Creature**
When Mantle Masher enters play, flip a Landscape in this Lane face down.
When Mantle Masher leaves play, flip it face up.
1 / 6

 **Man-Witch** — 2
**Useless Swamp Creature**
Whenever a foe discards a card, deal 1 Damage to that foe.
1 / 11

 **The Mariachi** — 2
**SandyLands Creature**
FLOOP >>> Deal 1 Damage to target Creature for each Creature that entered play this turn.
2 / 9

 **Master of Disguise** — 1
**Rainbow Spell**
Each of your opponent's Creatures has -1 ATK this turn.

 **Mausoleum** — 1
**Useless Swamp Building**
Your Creature in this Lane has +1 DEF for every 5 cards in your discard pile.

 **Mothball** — 1
**Useless Swamp Creature**
-2 DEF for every 5 cards in your discard pile.
2 / 4

 **Ms. Fluff** — 2
**NiceLands Creature**
While Ms. Fluff has exactly 2 Damage on it, it has +7 ATK.
2 / 10

 **Ms. Mummy** — 0
**Rainbow Creature**
At the start of your turn, you may return Ms. Mummy to its owner's hand. If you do, target SandyLand Creature you control gains 1 DEF.
1 / 4

 **Musical Chair** — 0
**Rainbow Spell**
Swap up to 2 of your Landscapes with ones from outside of the game.

 **Music Mallard** — 1
**NiceLands Creature**
FLOOP >>> Draw a card. If Music Mallard has 5 or more Damage on it, draw an additional card.
0 / 9

 **Nice Ice Baby** — 0
**Rainbow Creature**
+3 ATK while your opponent does not control a Creature in this Lane.
1 / 2

 **Nice Windmill** — 1
**NiceLands Building**
Pay 1 Action >>> Heal or deal up to 2 Damage to your Creature in this Lane.

 **Niceasaurus Rex** — 1
**NiceLands Creature**
At the start of your turn, if Niceasaurus Rex has Damage on it, draw a card.
2 / 7

 **Night Tower** — 1
**Useless Swamp Building**
FLOOP >>> If your opponent has no Creature in this Lane, they discard a card.

 **Ogre Braces** — 1
Useless Swamp Spell
You heal 1 Hit Point for every 5 cards in your discard pile.

 **Ogre Gas** — 0
Rainbow Spell
Reveal the top 3 cards of your deck. Put one of them on the bottom of your deck and discard the rest.

 **Oil Refinery** — 2
Blue Plains Building
Your Creature on this Landscape has +2 DEF for each Oil Refinery you control.

 **Ol' Corn Eye** — 2
Cornfield Creature
+1 DEF for each different Landscape type you control.
4 / 1

 **Orange Slimey** — 1
Useless Swamp Creature
If you control 3 or more different Landscape types when Orange Slimey enters play, deal 3 Damage to your opponent.
2 / 6

 **Palace of Bone** — 1
Useless Swamp Building
Opposing Creatures in this Lane don't trigger entering or leaving play effects.

 **Paladin** — 2
Blue Plains Creature
Each Creature that changed Lanes this turn has +3 ATK this turn. (Opposing Creatures do not benefit from this.)
3 / 7

 **Pants Of Awesome** — 1
Blue Plains Spell
Move target Creature you control to an empty Blue Plains Landscape you control, and then draw a card.

 **Papercut Tiger** — 2
NiceLands Creature
While Papercut Tiger has exactly 5 Damage on it, it has +5 ATK.
2 / 9

 **Parrotmilitary Outpost** — 0
Rainbow Building
Each Creature in this Lane has +1 ATK with Oil.

 **Patchy the Pumpkin** — 1
Cornfield Creature
FLOOP >>> Deal 1 Damage to target Creature. Do this once for each Cornfield Landscape you control. (May only target each Creature once.)
0 / 5

 **Peach Djinni** — 0
Rainbow Creature
When a SandyLand Creature enters play under your control, Peach Djinni has +1 ATK this turn.
0 / 6

 **Pentacutie** — 2
Blue Plains Creature
Opponents can't play 0-cost cards.
3 / 8

 **Pentaid** — 1
NiceLands Spell
Heal exactly 5 Damage from target Creature you control (no more and no less).

 **Phyllis** — 1
Rainbow Creature
While the blade distracts you, her purse swings in for the whammy.
2 / 7

 **Pickler** — 2
Useless Swamp Creature
Sacrifice Pickler >>> Deal 3 Damage to target Creature.
2 / 9

 **Pixelops** — 1
NiceLands Creature
When Pixelops enters play, heal 1 Damage from each adjacent Creature.
2 / 7

 **Pied Piper** — 2
Cornfield Creature
When Pied Piper attacks an opposing Creature, you may have a Flooped Creature you control attack it instead.
1 / 9

 **Piestorm** — 1
NiceLands Spell
Each of your Creatures with no Damage has +2 ATK this turn.

 **The Pig** — 1
Rainbow Creature
FLOOP >>> Flip target Cornfield Landscape in this Lane Face Down.
1 / 4

 **Pink Candy** — 1
Blue Plains Spell
Each of your Creatures has +2 ATK this turn while attacking a Creature that is on a SandyLands Landscape.

 **Pink Merwitch** — 2
Useless Swamp Creature
Discard a card >>> Deal 1 Damage to each opposing Creature. (Use only once during each of your turns.)
2 / 8

 **Pirate Bear** — 1
Cornfield Creature
While Pirate Bear is on a Useless Swamp Landscape, it deals triple Damage.
1 / 3

 **Polterclops** — 2
SandyLands Creature
+1 DEF for each different Landscape type you control.
4 / 1

 **Pony** — 0
Rainbow Creature
1 / 5

**Popcorn Butterfly** — 1

**Cornfield Creature**

Floop >>> Draw a card for each Building you control.

1 / 5

**Popcorn Power** — 1

**Cornfield Spell**

Each of your Creatures has +2 ATK this turn while attacking a Creature that is on a Blue Plains Landscape.

**Portal of Unsummoning** — 2

**SandyLands Spell**

Return target Creature to its owner's hand.

**Portal to Nowhere** — 1

**SandyLands Spell**

Move 1 of your opponent's Creatures to an adjacent empty Lane (on its side).

**Psionic Architect** — 1

**Blue Plains Creature**

When Psionic Architect enters play, you may ready a Flooped Creature you control.

2 / 6

**Psionic Swashbuckler** — 1

**Blue Plains Creature**

When Psionic Swashbuckler enters play, you may deal 3 Damage to target Flooped Creature.

2 / 6

**Psychic Tempest** — 1

**SandyLands Spell**

Return all Creatures in play you own to your hand. (This includes stolen Creatures.)

**Puma Paw** — 1

**Blue Plains Spell**

Ready a Flooped Creature you control. It has +2 ATK this turn.

**Punk Cat** — 1

**Blue Plains Creature**

Each Creature that changed Lanes this turn has +2 ATK this turn.

2 / 6

**Puppy Parade** — 2

**Blue Plains Spell**

Heal 2 Damage from each Creature you control. Creatures you control lose their Landscape type and become Rainbow Creatures this turn.

**Pyramidia** — 1

**Blue Plains Building**

FLOOP >>> If you control a Creature in this Lane, gain 1 Action. Use it only to play a Creature into this Lane.

**Quadurai** — 0

**Rainbow Creature**

At the start of your turn, deal 2 Damage to each opponent with 9 or more cards in hand.

0 / 6

**Quake Maker** — 1

**Cornfield Creature**

+2 ATK for each Face-down Landscape in play.

1 / 7

**Quick Pick Me Up** — 1

**SandyLands Spell**

Return target Creature you control to its owner's hand. Gain Actions equal to its cost.

**Rainbow Eyebat** — 1

**NiceLands Creature**

At the start of your turn, you heal 1 Hit Point for each different Landscape type you control. (Can't go over 25.)

1 / 4

**Raise the Dead** — 1

**Useless Swamp Spell**

Put a Creature with cost 2 or less from your discard pile into play.

**Rebounding Zebracorn** — 1

**Cornfield Creature**

+1 ATK for each different Landscape type you control.

0 / 6

**Reclaim Landscape** — 0

**Rainbow Spell**

You may flip one of your Landscapes Face up, and you may move one of your Buildings to one of your Lanes without one.

**Red Eyeling** — 1

**Useless Swamp Creature**

FLOOP >>> Return a card with cost 0 from your discard pile to your hand.

2 / 6

**Reign Deer** — 2

**IcyLands Creature**

FLOOP >>> Draw a card for each Landscape with a Frozen token on it players control.

4 / 4

**Ring of Damage** — 2

**Rainbow Spell**

Each of your Creatures has +2 ATK this turn.

**Ring Of Fluffy** — 2

**NiceLands Spell**

Target Creature you control has +X ATK this turn, where X is the amount of Damage on it.

**Ring of Third Eye** — 1

**Blue Plains Spell**

Each of your Creatures has +2 ATK this turn while attacking a Creature that is on a Cornfield Landscape.

**River of Swords** — 2

**Rainbow Spell**

Creatures you control each have +2 ATK this turn. Draw 2 cards.

**Rock 'n Roller** — 2

**Cornfield Creature**

When Rock 'n Roller enters play, Flip a Landscape in this Lane face down. When Rock 'n Roller leaves play, flip it Face up.

2 / 8

 **Rock Out!** — 0 — Rainbow Spell
Flip target Landscape face down until the start of your next turn.

 **Rocktopus** — 2 — Rainbow Creature
Rocktopus has +1 ATK while attacking a Creature that is on a SandyLands Landscape. 3/6

 **Sack of Pain** — 2 — NiceLands Creature
While Sack of Pain has exactly 6 Damage on it, it has +6 ATK. 2/10

 **Sand Angel** — 0 — Rainbow Creature
Lie down in the sand, wave your arms and legs, and she will appear to you. 1/5

 **Sand Eyebat** — 2 — SandyLands Creature
When another Creature enters play under your control, Sand Eyebat gains 1 DEF. 1/10

 **Sand Jackal** — 1 — SandyLands Creature
While Sand Jackal is on a NiceLands Landscape, when it defeats an opposing Creature, you heal 3 Hit Points. 3/3

 **Sand Knights** — 1 — SandyLands Creature
+2 ATK if you control a Blue Plains Landscape. 1/8

 **Sand Pyramid** — 1 — SandyLands Building
Pay 2 Actions >>> Return each Creature in this Lane to its owner's hand. (Affects both players.)

 **Sand Sphinx** — 2 — SandyLands Building
FLOOP >>> Return a Creature you control in this Lane to its owner's hand.

 **Sandhorn Devil** — 1 — SandyLands Creature
When Sandhorn Devil enters play, deal 1 Damage to each Creature in play (including each of your Creatures). 3/6

 **Sandasaurus Rex** — 2 — SandyLands Creature
+2 ATK for each of your empty Landscapes. 0/9

 **Sandmagus** — 1 — SandyLands Creature
At the start of your turn, you may return Sandmagus to its owner's hand. If you do, each other Creature you control -1 ATK this turn. 2/4

 **Sandsnake** — 1 — SandyLands Creature
When Sandsnake enters play, deal 4 Damage to target opposing Creature in this Lane. 0/9

 **SandWitch** — 1 — SandyLands Creature
When SandWitch or another Creature enters play under your control, deal 1 Damage to your opponent. 0/12

 **Schoolhouse** — 1 — Blue Plains Building
FLOOP >>> Your Creature in this Lane loses all abilities and gains the FLOOP ability of a random Creature with a FLOOP ability in your discard pile until end of turn.

 **Scroll of Bad Breath** — 1 — Useless Swamp Spell
Each of your Creatures has +2 ATK this turn while attacking a Creature that is on a NiceLands Landscape.

 **Scroll of Fresh Breath** — 1 — NiceLands Spell
Each of your Creatures has +2 ATK this turn while attacking a Creature that is on a Useless Swamp Landscape.

 **Sea Hag** — 2 — Rainbow Creature
Sea Hag has +1 ATK while attacking a Creature that is on a Useless Swamp Landscape. 3/6

 **Shadowy Pyramid** — 1 — Useless Swamp Building
FLOOP >>> Draw a card. If you control a Creature in this Lane, discard a card.

 **Shark** — 2 — SandyLands Creature
When a SandyLand Creature enters play during your turn (including Shark), it has +1 ATK this turn. 2/10

 **Sharp Guy** — 1 — Cornfield Creature
Floop >>> Deal 2 Damage to target opposing Creature in this Lane. 1/5

 **Silo of Freedom** — 1 — Cornfield Building
Discard a card >>> Your Landscape in this Lane loses its type and becomes the type of your choice (except Face down) until the start of your next turn.

 **Silo of Justice** — 1 — Cornfield Building
Pay 1 Action >>> Deal 1 Damage to target Creature in this Lane and 1 Damage to its controller.

 **Silo of Truth** — 1 — Cornfield Building
Pay 2 Actions >>> Steal a random card from your opponent's hand and play it at no cost.

 **Singing Sword** — 0 — Rainbow Spell
Target Creature has +1 ATK this turn for every 2 cards you have drawn this turn.

**Sinkhole** — 2
Cornfield Building
Discard a card, FLOOP >>> Flip target Landscape in this Lane face down until the start of your next turn.

**Ska-pion** — 1
SandyLands Creature
Ska-pion costs 1 less to play while an opponent controls a Creature you own.
3 / 3

**Skeletal Hand** — 2
Useless Swamp Creature
FLOOP >>> Discard the top 3 cards of your deck. For each Spell discarded this way, target players discards a card.
3 / 6

**Slay Rider** — 1
IcyLands Creature
FLOOP >>> Deal 3 Damage to target Creature on a Landscape with a Frozen token on it.
0 / 5

**The Sludger** — 1
Useless Swamp Creature
FLOOP >>> Choose a card name. Remove each card with that name in target players discard pile from the game.
1 / 8

**Smoldering Elder** — 2
Useless Swamp Creature
When Smoldering Elder enters play, each players discards 2 cards.
3 / 8

**Snake Eye Ring** — 0
Rainbow Spell
Return a random Useless Swamp Creature from your discard pile to your hand.

**Snake Eyes** — 1
SandyLands Spell
Each of your Creatures has +2 ATK this turn while attacking a Creature that is on a Useless Swamp Landscape.

**Snakemint** — 1
NiceLands Creature
When Snakemint deals Damage to an opposing player, you heal that many Hit Points. (Can't go over 25.)
1 / 7

**Snow Angel** — 1
IcyLands Creature
FLOOP >>> Heal 1 Damage from each of your Creatures for each Landscape with a Frozen token on it players control.
2 / 7

**Snow Baller** — 1
IcyLands Creature
Remove a Frozen token from Snow Baller's Landscape >>> Deal 3 Damage to target Creature.
2 / 7

**Snow Bunny** — 1
IcyLands Creature
Destroy Snow Bunny >>> Freeze target Landscape.
3 / 3

**Snow Business** — 2
IcyLands Building
Pay 1 Action >>> Freeze target Landscape in this Lane.

**Snow Dog** — 2
IcyLands Creature
FLOOP >>> Each adjacent Creature has +2 ATK this turn.
2 / 7

**Snow Training Camp** — 0
Rainbow Building
FLOOP >>> Freeze both Landscapes in this Lane. Use only if no Frozen tokens are in play.

**Snow Way** — 1
IcyLands Spell
Freeze two target Landscapes.

**Snowblower** — 1
IcyLands Spell
Choose a Lane. Freeze both Landscapes in that Lane.

**Snowvalanche** — 0
Rainbow Spell
Deal 2 Damage to each opposing Creature on a Landscape with a Frozen token on it.

**Socks of Fortitude** — 1
Blue Plains Spell
Ready each Creature that changed Lanes this turn. They each have +2 ATK this turn.

**Spazzy Cola** — 0
Rainbow Spell
Each Creature in play has +1 ATK this turn including your opponent's Creatures!

**Spell Warp** — 1
Blue Plains Spell
Swap the position of 2 Creatures you control. (They change Lanes simultaneously!)

**Spike Icicle** — 0
Rainbow Creature
Look out below!
3 / 1

**Spirit Tower** — 2
Useless Swamp Building
Pay 1 Action and FLOOP >>> If you control no Creatures in this Lane, move target Creature in this Lane to your side and ready it. At end of turn, return it to its owner's side.

**Sprucy Lucy** — 2
IcyLands Creature
Sprucy Lucy has +1 ATK for each Landscape with a Frozen token on it players control.
2 / 9

**Squatting Bald Man** — 1
Useless Swamp Creature
Discard a card >>> Heal 1 Damage from Squatting Bald Man. (Use any number of times during each of your turns!)
2 / 7

 **Static Parrotrooper** — 0
Rainbow Creature
When Static Parrotrooper enters play, move it to any empty Landscape. It cannot be replaced.
At the start of your turn, deal 1 Damage to your Hero.
0 / 6

 **Steakchop** — 1
Useless Swamp Creature
At the start of your turn, Discard 2 cards or destroy Steakchop. (Discard after your free draw.)
4 / 4

 **Strawberry Slimey** — 1
NiceLands Creature
If you control 3 or more different Landscape types when Strawberry Slimey enters play, heal 4 Damage from each Creature you control.
2 / 6

 **Strength Crystal** — 2
Blue Plains Spell
Target player draws five cards.

 **Struzann Jinn** — 2
Blue Plains Creature
+2 ATK for each Flooped Creature you control.
1 / 11

 **Subliminal Strength** — 1
Blue Plains Spell
Target Creature you control has +2 ATK this turn for each Spell you played this turn (including this one!)

 **Sun King**
Cornfield Creature
Sun King counts as an additional Cornfield Landscape you control.
0 / 8

 **Sundae School** — 1
Rainbow Building
While you have an even amount of Hit Points, your Creature on this Landscape has +2 ATK.

 **Swamp Horn** — 2
Useless Swamp Creature
+1 DEF for each different Landscape type you control.
4 / 1

 **Sword Bouquet** — 1
Rainbow Spell
Deal 1 Damage to target Creature for every card you have drawn this turn.

 **Tapped Out** — 1
Blue Plains Spell
Target Creature you control has +2 ATK for each exhausted Creature you control (at the time you play this!)

 **Tax Reduction** — 1
Blue Plains Spell
You may move each of your Buildings to different Lanes you control.
You may move each of your opponent's Buildings to different Lanes he controls.

 **Teeth Leaf** — 2
Useless Swamp Creature
If you have 10 or more cards in your discard pile, pay 2 fewer Actions to play Teeth Leaf.
3 / 10

 **Teleport** — 0
Rainbow Spell
Move one of your Creatures to one of your empty Lanes.

 **Temple of the Sun** — 1
SandyLands Building
When a SandyLands Creature with cost 1 or greater you control enters play in this Lane, you may return it to its owner's hand.

 **Timmy Magic Eyes** — 2
Rainbow Creature
Timmy Magic Eyes has +1 ATK while attacking a Creature that is on a Blue Plains Landscape.
3 / 6

 **Tiny Elephant** — 1
Blue Plains Creature
While in play, Tiny Elephant is also a Rainbow Creature. (In addition to Blue Plains.)
2 / 6

 **Tired Wombat** — 2
Blue Plains Creature
At the start of your turn, move Tired Wombat to an empty Landscape you control. If you cannot, move it to an empty Landscape your opponent controls.
4 / 6

 **TNTimmy** — 0
Rainbow Creature
When TNTimmy leaves play, deal 1 Damage to each opposing Creature.
0 / 5

 **Toilet Of Doom** — 1
Useless Swamp Spell
Target Creature you control has +1 ATK this turn for every 5 cards in your discard pile.

 **Tome of Ankhs** — 1
SandyLands Spell
Draw a card for each of your empty Lanes.

 **Tornado Wall Of Fire** — 2
Cornfield Creature
Floop >>> Tornado Wall of Fire has +3 ATK while Flooped.
0 / 10

 **Tough Lumberjill** — 2
Cornfield Creature
When Tough Lumberjill enters play, deal 1 Damage to your opponent for each Building you control.
3 / 6

 **Travelin' Farmer** — 2
Cornfield Creature
When Travelin' Farmer enters play, deal 1 Damage to your opponent for each card in his hand.
2 / 12

 **Travelin' Skeleton** — 1
Blue Plains Creature
FLOOP >>> Travelin' Skeleton and another Creature you control change Lanes with each other.
0 / 8

**Travelin' Wizard** — 2 — Blue Plains Creature
When Travelin' Wizard enters play, the opposing Creature in this Lane and Travelin' Wizard switch sides.
3 / 3

**Tree of Undeath** — 2 — Useless Swamp Creature
FLOOP >>> Return a random Creature from your discard pile to your hand.
2 / 6

**Unempty Coffin** — 0 — Rainbow Spell
Reduce the cost of the next Creature you play this turn by 2 Actions.

**Unicyclops** — 2 — Useless Swamp Creature
At the start of your turn, each player draws a card and then discards a card.
1 / 10

**Uni-Knight** — 1 — Blue Plains Creature
Pay 1 Action >>> Target Creature in this Lane has -10 ATK this turn.
3 / 4

**Vampire Lord** — 2 — Rainbow Creature
When Vampire Lord deals damage, heal that much Damage from him.
1 / 8

**Void Thimble** — 0 — Rainbow Spell
Lose 2 Hit Points, gain 1 Action.

**Volcano** — 1 — Rainbow Spell
Destroy target Building. You may deal 3 Damage to a Creature in that Lane. Flip your Landscape in that Lane Face down.

**Wake Up Call** — 1 — Blue Plains Spell
Ready each Creature you control.

**Wall Of Chocolate** — 2 — NiceLands Creature
While Wall of Chocolate has no Damage on it, it has +3 ATK.
1 / 9

**Wall of Ears** — 1 — Cornfield Creature
+1 DEF for each Cornfield Landscape in play (counting all players).
2 / 4

**Wall of Sand** — 2 — SandyLands Creature
If one or more other SandyLand Creatures enter play during your turn, Wall of Sand has +2 ATK this turn.
1 / 12

**Wandering Bald Man** — 0 — Rainbow Creature
At the start of your turn, put the top card of your deck into your discard pile.
0 / 10

**Weakened Warrior** — 2 — Blue Plains Creature
Weakened Warrior comes into play exhausted and does not ready at the start of your turn. Whenever Weakened Warrior changes Lanes, ready it.
5 / 6

**Weary Trading Post** — 0 — Rainbow Building
FLOOP >>> Move an exhausted Creature you control to this Landscape (if empty).

**Well-Dressed Wolf** — 2 — Rainbow Creature
Well-Dressed Wolf has +1 ATK while attacking a Creature that is on a Cornfield Landscape.
3 / 6

**Windmill Of Health** — 1 — NiceLands Building
While your Creature in this Lane has no Damage on it, it has +2 ATK.

**Witch Slap** — 2 — Rainbow Spell
Target opponent discards down to 5 cards, and then takes 1 Damage for each card discarded this way.

**Witch Way** — 1 — Cornfield Spell
Each of your Creatures that is on a Useless Swamp Landscape has +2 ATK this turn.

**Woad Blood** — 0 — Rainbow Spell
Each Creature that changed Lanes this turn has +2 ATK this turn.

**Woad Mobile Home** — 1 — Blue Plains Building
FLOOP >>> Move a Creature in an adjacent Lane to this Lane (if empty).

**Woad Talisman** — 0 — Rainbow Spell
Target Blue Plains Creature you control has +2 ATK this turn.

**Woadic Chief** — 2 — Blue Plains Creature
Woadic Chief has +2 ATK this turn for each Spell you have played this turn.
2 / 10

**Woadic Marauder** — 2 — Blue Plains Creature
When Woadic Marauder changes Lanes during a turn, draw a card.
3 / 9

**Woadic Enchantress** — 2 — Blue Plains Creature
Creatures in this Lane cannot use Floop abilities.
2 / 10

**Woadie Matriarch**
1
Blue Plains Creature
Woadie Matriarch has +1 ATK for each Rainbow Creature you control.
1 / 7

**Woadie Ring Leader**
1
Blue Plains Creature
At the start of your turn, move Woadie Ring Leader to an empty Landscape you control. If you cannot, destroy it.
3 / 4

**Woadie Weirdo**
1
Blue Plains Creature
Floop >>> Reveal a card from your hand. That card becomes a Rainbow card until the end of your turn.
(If has no Landscape type.)
1 / 7

**X-Large Spirit Soldier**
1
Blue Plains Creature
Each adjacent Creature has +1 ATK.
1 / 9

**Yellow Gnome**
1
Cornfield Creature
FLOOP >>> Deal 1 Damage to each opposing Creature that is on a NiceLands Landscape.
1 / 6

**Yellow Lighthouse**
1
Cornfield Building
At the start of your turn, each player who controls a Creature in this Lane draws a card.

**Yellow Slimey**
1
Cornfield Creature
While you control 3 or more different Landscape types, Yellow Slimey has +3 ATK.
0 / 6

**ZaZo's Magic Seeds**
0
Rainbow Spell
Target SandyLand Creature has +2 ATK this turn for each Creature that entered play into an adjacent Lane this turn.